T0129759

ALSO BY THE AUTHOR

A Journey of Faith. Moving From the Middle East to The West. Living in Two Different Cultures. iUniverse, Bloomington, IN, 2011.

Two Different Religions. How Islam Perceives Christianity and What is The Truth. Authorhouse, Bloomington, IN, 2013.

About Learning and Education. A Parent and Educator's View Supported by Overseas Experience. Dawlat Bishara, Co-author. Authorhouse, Bloomington, IN, 2015.

God, Power, and Man. Dawlat Bishara, Co-author. Authorhouse, Bloomington, IN, 2018.

SMART!
WHAT DO YOU MEAN?
MARVELS OF THE HUMAN MIND

Dr. Safwat Bishara, Ph. D.
Dr. Dawlat Bishara, Ph. D.

authorHOUSE®

AuthorHouse™
1663 Liberty Drive
Bloomington, IN 47403
www.authorhouse.com
Phone: 1 (800) 839-8640

Published by AuthorHouse 11/29/2019

ISBN: 978-1-7283-3791-3 (sc)
ISBN: 978-1-7283-3790-6 (hc)
ISBN: 978-1-7283-3792-0 (e)

Library of Congress Control Number: 2019919500

Print information available on the last page.

Contents

Epigraph

ROMANS, 7:14-15 says For we know that the law is spiritual: but I am carnal, sold under sin. For that which I do I allow not: for what I would, that do I not; but what I hate, that do I.

Acknowledgment

The authors would like to thank Stacy Martin for editing this work. Her efforts and time are greatly appreciated.

INTRODUCTION

The brain is "the most magnificent structure on this earth," said Dr. Marian Diamond (1926 – 2017), WALL STREET JOURNAL, Saturday/Sunday, August 5-6, 2017, p. A5. This three-pound lump of cells could conjure thoughts and ideas; store and categorize information for years; think and invent new theories; build computers with extraordinary capacities to execute thousands and millions of commands and mathematical calculations almost instantly.

Dr. Diamond's research on rats, published in 1964, provided evidence that helped by doing away with the notion that mental capacity is fixed from birth and is bound to weaken appreciably with age. Her advice is "Use it or lose it."

Physiology aside, human behavior also falls under the control of the mind. Ravi Zacharias, the renowned contemporary Christian apologist, writes "Thought is the precursor to action." THE END OF REASON, Zondervan, Grand Rapids, Michigan, 2008, 64. Dr. James Merritt, in his sermon broadcast on July 8, 2018, puts it this way "The mind is the command or control center of the body. We must guide our mind in all things."

How can we guard our minds against negative influence

propagated mostly by ever popular entertainment tools from the television to the Internet to social media? The Word of God addresses the topic in three areas.

First, we must *guide* our mind in all things. II CORINTHIANS, 10:3-4 says For though we walk in the flesh, we do not war after the flesh: For the weapons of our warfare are not carnal, but mighty through God to the pulling down of strong holds.

The soul is the moral compass; the heart is the source of emotions; the body is the physical boundary; and the mind is the spiritual center.

Second, we must *guard* our minds against wrong things. II CORINTHIANS, 10: 5 says Casting down imaginations, and every high thing that exalteth itself against the knowledge of God, and bringing into captivity every thought to the obedience of Christ.

To man, the mind is like a castle. Satan's attacks go straight to the bull's eye. An evil thought left unchecked is likely to fester and grow, and may eventually be acted upon. From just a thought to an act proceeds quietly with Satan making justifications to gloss over the consequences while pushing forward the wrong idea.

EPHESIANS, 6: 12 says For we wrestle not against flesh and blood, but against principalities, against powers, against the rulers of the darkness of this world, against spiritual wickedness in high places. EPHESIANS, 6:16 tells us Above all, taking the shield of faith, wherewith ye shall be able to quench all the fiery darts of the wicked.

Third, we must feed our mind the *right* things. COLOSSIANS, 3: 2,3 says Set your affection on things above, not on things on the earth. For ye are dead, and your life is hid with Christ in God.

PHILIPPIANS, 4: 8 tells us Finally, bretheren, whatsoever things are true, whatsoever things are honest, whatsoever things are just, whatsoever things are pure, whatsoever things are lovely, whatsoever things are of good report; if there be any virtue, and if there be any praise, think on these things.

How beautiful, insightful, and perfect is the Word of our Lord.

CHAPTER 1

GOOD AND EVIL. CAN THEY COEXIST?

Angels worship and execute God's will on earth. Satan and his dominions seek to destroy man's life—literally and figuratively. Human beings fall in between. Each one of us is a mixture of good and evil, whereas we differ only in the proportion of each. Our human nature favors and tend towards evil that comes naturally to man. To be good, and to do good, takes determination rooted in the belief of a loving and merciful God.

God created man. Man has been given dominion on all created things: "fish of the sea, ...the fowl of the air, … the cattle, all the earth, … every creeping thing that creepeth upon the earth," GENESIS, 1: 26.

In paradise, man sinned. Satan deceived Adam and Eve into disobeying God's instructions. Evil entered the world, and the second generation saw Cain slew his brother Abel.

The battle between good and evil, between morality and sin, between G-rated [G = God] and R-rated life styles continues.

The battlefield of the war between good and evil is, as it has always been, in the human mind. It is the command and control center of the body. The great deceiver plants an evil seed in man's mind. Unless one guards his mind man starts to contemplate the idea, and may even find a justification to carry on. Allowing the thought to drag on is a lost battle that Satan eventually wins.

The Creator, in His love for man, has provided the instructions on choosing the right path.

But can we captivate *all* of our thoughts? Few are able. Few totally fail. Most of us fall in between with alternating decisions that verge on the side of good or evil. Born in sin, man's heart has been contaminated. Ravi Zacharias, Ibid., 68 explains "I recall Malcolm Muggeridge once having remarked that the depravity of the human heart is at once the most intellectually resisted yet most empirically verifiable reality. Wickedness is always excused as anything but the moral degeneracy that has resulted from each one of us becoming the god of God."

Sally Beauman eloquently presents the case for an individual, a young girl named Constance, who embodied both good and evil. Now one might wonder what is so special about Constance, aren't we all the product of both good and evil coexisting together but in different proportions?

In her novel DARK ANGEL, Bantam Books, New York, Toronto, London, Sydney, Auckland, 1990, 786 pages, Beauman tells about the life of an aristocratic British family that spans most of the twentieth century. All reference citations in this chapter are from Beauman's book.

The family fortunes go back to the great-great-grandfather

of Victoria (the novel's narrator) who made a fortune "first from soap and then from patent bleaches." Victoria's great-grandfather "made even more money from his bleaches and his factories" situated in Scotland. But he apparently preferred "not to be reminded of bleach," so he moved his family south to Winterscombe estates, went into politics, purchased a barony, and became the first Lord Callendar, and sent my grandfather, Denton Cavendish, to Eton." Ibid., 33.

Denton, sixty five, is married to an American named Gwen. At thirty-eight she is a remarkably handsome woman. The four sons: Boy, Freddie, Acland, and Steenie lived at Winterscombe where King Edward VII has stayed on one occasion. Boy was eighteen and has left school. Freddie is powerfully built, wide-shouldered, and square hipped; "his temper blazed quietly, then dies away and is forgotten." Acland was so quick, so bright, so strong and unpredictable, so fierce and sudden in his passions." He raced after more information, he must always understand— and "this pursuit of his ... made him hectic." Ibid., 88-91.

In April 1910 Halley's comet would be sighted. The sighting of the comet was an excuse for Gwen to have a party.

Gwen's lover, Edward Shawcross, was invited among others to the party. Eddie was a writer whose wife, Jessica, had died of tuberculosis in a Swiss sanitarium leaving him a two-year daughter named Constance.

Boy considered Shawcross almost as a member of the family based on his well established friendship. But Acland, deeply loved by his mother, started to grow away from her.

"If he needed solace he no longer turned to his mother, and by the time he was twelve the break was complete." Ibid., 92. It turned out that Acland has noticed the relationship between his mother and Shawcross.

Another person also became aware of the illicit love affair. It was Constance who enjoyed spying, hiding, and listening behind closed doors.

The father-daughter relationship between Constance, ten years at the time, and her father was troubled in the least and destroyed in reality. Shawcross treated his motherless daughter coldly, almost cruelly. He mocked his daughter in front of friends. Shawcross refers to her simply as 'the albatross,' and sometimes "mimic the weight of that ill-omened bird around his neck." Ibid., 100. Constance must have been very lonely.

Boy, the eldest son, considered Constance to be an object of pity to be tolerated during her short visits to Winterscombe. But to be friendly with Constance is not easy. She repels pity. Whenever Constance feels someone's pity she deflects it at once. "Her manner is abrupt, prickly, rude. She seems to have unerring instincts for the weaknesses of others; she hones in on those weaknesses at once." Ibid., 99.

Boy likes photography. He suggested to Constance his desire to take a picture of her using his new Adams Videx camera. She clambered up onto the bed, legs swinging, and her skirts hitched up. Boy told Constance to be absolutely still to allow for long exposure because light is poor in the room. Under the hood he "reaches for the shutter bulb, adjusts the aperture. A half-second before the bulb is pressed, too late for Boy to stop, the child alters her position … she parted her thighs and … posed with her left hand lying across her thigh, her fingers outstretched pointing downward into her lap …. It is also (coupled with brazenness of her stare) the lewdest, the most lascivious gesture Boy has ever seen." Ibid., 101.

Denton, the household, loved pheasants and had many on his estate. But poachers repeatedly attacked the flock in his woods making Denton angry. He passionately believed in the sanctity of property. The decision was made to have traps in the woods—traps not just for animals. Man-traps are to catch the poachers: "steel traps with jagged jaws that close on a man's leg." Ibid., 120. There are also pit traps, with sharpened staves.

Constance father, Shawcross, has conflicting emotions regarding the Denton's family and their invited guests. He knows that they have money but he does not. He feels to be superior to them in every way, yet "they look down on him—he senses it." Ibid., 141. Out of politeness they "smile at his jokes …. They even listen attentively to his stories … but Shawcross knows he does not really engage them."

Constance appearance adds to her father's misery. She is filthy. Her father notices that her hair is tangled and uncombed; "her dress, torn at the helm, is muddied; she has not washed her hands, and her nails … are black." Ibid., 142.

Out of the four sons of Gwen, Steenie, the youngest, actually likes Constance. They were approximately the same age.

One of the regular guests at Winterscombe is the financier, Sir Montague Stern: a cultured, intelligent, and sophisticated man. A Jew who came—or so rumors say—from "the humblest origins, and though he may have risen high, very high, he can not leave those origins, racial and social, behind."

On the other hand, Shawcross despises Jews, women, and the working class just as he despises Irish and any person with a dark skin.

Later in the evening the party is in full swing. All excited and in anticipation of sighting Halley's comet that night in April 1910. Many people went outside on the terrace at Winterscombe gazing up at the night sky.

Acland glimpses the comet first and points. All around him people crane their necks, mill, and push. "The comet arcs; the stars pale; the darkness flares; the great trajectory is silent." Ibid., 154.

That night Gwen was to meet Shawcross at the clearing—a place in the woods. Gwen, however, felt guilty about her relationship with Constance's father. At the appointed time of midnight Shawcross walked through the path in the woods leading to the clearing where he waited for Gwen. She never came, and stayed on her knees by Steenie's bed who suffered from a fever that caused "his throat to swell so badly that he could not swallow saliva, let alone water." Ibid., 165.

As we shall see later, Gwen's change of heart towards sin will save her life. Was it a divine intervention, through the Holy Spirit, that awakened her conscious at the right moment?

On the other hand, Shawcross's fate was different.

Cattermole, Denton's land keeper, woke up early as

usual the next morning to patrol the estate. He checks his gun, and let two of the dogs out of their kennel.

Cattermole goes through his usual daily routine. He "quarters the woods, then makes for the clearing … where he has a quiet five-minute smoke." Ibid., 170. But this morning he notices an odd little mound in the grass—a mound that was not there the previous morning. The dogs start barking.

On his way to meet Gwen at the clearing after midnight of the comet party, Shawcross stumbles on one of the traps intended to catch trespassers. His right leg fragmented. "Below the knee it is twisted and foreshortened. One foot, shoeless, is bent up under his body; the shinbone, snapped in two places, protrudes through the flesh." The hands, arms, face are lacerated and "gobbets of blood spewed from his mouth; his lips are retracted … he appears to snarl." Ibid., 174. "The nails on his hands are ripped, … the stumps of his fingers are black with congealed blood; the hands are clenched like claws."

Cattermole, together with other men, put the body on a stretcher to carry home. With his face blanched with shock he tells the family that Shawcross must have been trapped for hours before he found him. He was alive when Cattermole and the other men got him out.

What a terrible way to die. Every human being is subject to death. But Shawcross has suffered terribly just before his death. Trapped for hours by the sharpened jaws of a trap he tried desperately to free his leg, but the more he tried, the more the jaws nipped at his body.

Was it a random event? Just one of the many ways for a man to die? Perhaps. There is no way to know or understand.

But Constance, his only daughter, who became motherless at the age of two, tells of her early years living with her own father. (After growing up sufficiently to write her journals, she describes how her father repeatedly abused her sexually. The abuse at her early years as a child undoubtedly had a lot to do with her troubled life as a teenager, adult, wife, godmother, and ended up with Constance taking her own life.)

What a man sows he reaps, just as the Word of God says. Constance father committed adultery with his host's wife, Gwen, and topped it up by sexually abusing his own child.

Yes, God is a loving God but He is also fair and just in His judgment. Shawcross did not show any remorse or felt guilty about his behavior.

Shawcross's corpse laid wrapped in a bundle of rugs. His "body … is so badged with blood that at first Gwen can not locate the source of the injuries, can not recognize the man before her." Ibid., 174.

Suddenly Constance swoops down upon the group by the stretcher. She rushed toward the rugs, onto the stretcher, unto the body. Her scream was both "terrifying and primitive … a scream of anger and grief …. Father, she cries, and then again, shaking him, Papa." Ibid., 175.

Constance looks up and stares in accusation at those around her: at Gwen, at Acland, at Boy, at Freddie, at Cattermole. "You killed him, she cries …You killed my father." Ibid., 175.

Having lost her father too, the motherless Constance

became an orphan. A decision has to be made as to where she would live, and with whom. Shawcross seemed to have virtually no family. The nearest family still alive were his mother's sister and her husband who had a small business in a small city. When contacted they made it clear that "their means were slender … they could not be made responsible for a child they had never met." Ibid., 190.

Gwen tells Constance that the Cavendish family feels responsible for her and that she will always have a home with them at Winterscombe. Constance has been expecting this, but understood that the invitation springs from a feeling of guilt not affection.

Showcross's death was claimed to be an accident. The inquiry was not too thorough. Not one member of the Cavendish family appeared at the inquest. Written evidence sufficed.

The local police had no intention of "offending such a prominent landowner as Lord Callendar whose cousin was Chief Constable of the County and whose closest friends were so prominent on the local judiciary." Ibid., 186.

In the trial, the jury was composed of local people, several of them were tenant farmers from the Cavendish estates. The verdict came as no surprise: Death by misadventure.

Constance will be living with the family (Denton, Gwen, Boy, Freddie, Acland, and Steenie) all the time, not just for a few weeks a year. Of the four sons only Steenie was delighted—Constance was about his age. The three older brothers were dismayed. But this did not deter Constance from hugging Steenie then solemnly advancing upon each of his three brothers to give each a kiss. She was poised, her small sharp chin tilted, apparently the very model of a dutiful and loving child. But was she?

Acland was fascinated by Constance. Sometimes he resented this feeling. He liked to "see her patterns shift, re-form, and scintillate … There must be a finite number of these patterns, but the speed and dazzle with which they altered and re-formed pleased him; he preferred to believe they were infinite, and infinitely arbitrary." Ibid., 207.

Four years have passed since her father's death. Constance greatly changed. She was small, fierce, quick, unpredictable, and possessed formidable energy. Her thick black hair was coarse and abundant giving her the appearance of a Gypsy. Constance never learned to be ladylike. Her hands always moved whether she was running, sitting, standing, or talking.

Acland noticed how Constance can make provocative transition from young woman to a young girl. She spied on Acland and found out about his relationship with Jenna—Constance maid, and this upset him.

Freddie liked to receive presents. Being at the center of attention, he could escape the need to compete with Steenie's dramatics or Acland's wit. Constance promised the 19-year-old Freddie a present—a proper present not in public at a party but *later.* His mind started to tingle as he thought about Constance words: 'Proper present,' and 'Later.' Freddie felt that familiar "ache of expectation, that lassitude and alerting … Constance now produced this effect upon him very easily." Ibid., 230.

This began soon after the death of Constance father, which meant it has been going on for four years. But it started in such small ways and it crept upon him in a subtle manner that Freddie was not even sure of how it got there. It was step by step, inch by inch, meeting by meeting to the point where he felt that Constance laid siege to him.

Is it wicked magic? Separate occasions blurred and commingled in Freddie's mind. Some were innocent and some less innocent. He never felt sure of when or what Constance said or did. All he knew was that, when Constance wanted, she had him in thrall. She teased Freddie's body, parts of his body, but also teased his mind, and his imagination which was why she was so powerful.

Constance wanted to take Freddie to Acland's room to be alone. Freddie hesitated. What if Acland came to his room and found them? Constance urged Freddie on by saying "you want your present, don't you?"

Freddie did want his present very much. His mind was about to explode with the possibilities of that present.

But Constance took Freddie first to Boy's room. She went to the wooden cabinet where Boy kept his photographs. She produced a key from her pocket, unlocked and then opened the last of the cabinet drawers. Constance showed Freddie pictures Boy took of her when she was younger. In some, she looked like a prostitute. The poses gave the impression that Constance continued to look both deprived and depraved. In some pictures Constance was shown where a sly hand would draw attention to a forbidden part of her anatomy. In others she parted her legs to show a cleft in plump flesh.

Astonished, Freddie stared at the pictures. Sickness crawled in his stomach. The photographs disgusted and appalled him; they also aroused him (and this made him feel shameful).

Constance told Freddie that it started when she was ten, before the death of her father, and it stopped when she was nearly thirteen. Although she promised Boy that she would never breathe a word to a soul, she said to Freddie I thought you ought to see so you would know your brother isn't quite what he seems.

To Acland room Constance went and Freddie followed her. He stood at the foot of the bed while she slowly stretched.

"Where should Freddie look first? … At her red lips, which were parted very slightly …. At her breasts … at her flat and boyish stomach? … [he] looked at all these things, all these components of Constance wicked magic …. she frowned, passed her tongue across her lips, bit the tip of her tongue … [then] began to touch herself." Ibid., 235.

Suddenly she ordered Freddie to open the door which he did after a little hesitation. He asked to touch her but she pushed his hand aside. Constance continued to rub her finger against herself till her body "shuddered, jerked, and then was still."

Boy enlisted in the war just like many others including the servants who were encouraged by Denton to join up. Acland was in London at the Foreign Office. Only Freddie stayed at Winterscombe. Gwen escorted Freddie to a famous Harley Street specialist recommended by financier Montague Stern. After a thorough and exhaustive physical examination the specialist looked grim. He said it is quite out of the question for Freddie to join up. If conscription ever came, he would be exempt because of a slight irregularity in the heart valves.

Gwen felt relieved. With two sons already away from home and involved in the war she just couldn't bear the agony of having another son's fate uncertain.

Freddie's obsession with Constance grew stronger. She was his confidance and his counselor. Constance, "experimenting with techniques that she was later to use to even greater effect, was an artist in sex. She understood that hints, promises, and caprice, delays and deviations were a more effective drug than fulfillment." Ibid., 240.

Freddie discovered that Constance favorite game was to risk danger when one of his family was nearby.

During the years that followed her father's death Constance tried to portray that her childhood had been anything but happy. She claimed that she loved her father as well as the Cavendish family with whom she lived after being orphaned. Constance hated to admit weakness. (Her journals, however, later revealed she was on the verge of mental breakdown.) She has long suspected that her father was murdered by someone tied up to Winterscombe: a member of the host family, a guest, a worker.

In 1915 Constance became ill. She refused to eat, went through rapid physical decline and had severely troubled sleep. Freddie believed that the past had poisoned him as well as Constance. Because she could not force the past out of her system, "since there was no emetic for a poison of this kind, Constance was willing herself to die." Ibid., 262.

But in a few weeks Constance recovered and persevered. She had a strong willpower.

One sunny day Gwen, Freddie, Jane Conyngham, Acland, Steenie, and Constance went for a stroll in Hyde Park. Constance brought her dog Floss with her. He raced back and forth, and rolled in the grass.

Some horse riders were also in the park. As the horses came closer Floss saw Constance on the far side of the sand track. He ran to join her. Freddie doubted that the riders saw him. Floss was tangled in the horses' hooves who were just moving at a canter but it was enough. He was tossed up in the air, a small bundle of fur. He was dead, his neck broken before he hit the ground.

Constance carried him all the way home. She cried. She clutched Floss tight and no one could persuade her to relinquish him.

Acland carried Constance into the house and Gwen put her in bed. She remained in bed the next day and the day after. She did not eat but took some water. As if intent on punishing herself more, she ceased speaking. Day after day her condition worsened.

Acland felt he has to face Constance. He came into her room, put his arm under her shoulders and lifted her. With a mirror in his hand he propped her against the pillows and said: "Look. Can you see? Look at yourself, Constance."

"The face choked her. It was the face of no one she knew. It was ashen; the bones stood out sharply; there were sores around the mouth; the eyes were sunken, ringed with shadows."
Ibid., 270.

Acland pulled back the covers and said: 'I want you

out of bed.' He picked her up and took her to the window then out onto the small iron balcony. After a little while Constance asked Acland to take her inside. He did not move, and instead gave her a cruel shake that jarred every bone in her body. The decisive moment came when he said "you are killing yourself … and expect that everyone will stand by and let you do it. I won't …. So, you shall choose …. Either you go back inside and begin living or I will simply let go of you …. Forty feet down. You will feel nothing. You decide." Ibid., 272.

Much later that night Constance had taken some food. She felt new and stronger. It was after this incident that she told Acland how often she disliked and hated herself. She thought that she damaged people and can not explain it. "I am not always like that. Sometimes I almost feel I might be good …. But then—something happens. I change, and I have to do harm." Ibid., 274.

How marvelous is the human mind! Sometimes it can be kept under control, and often seems to have its own 'mind.' Constance, the DARK ANGEL, oscillated between good and evil. She, like most, could not understand her behavior. When Floss, her first dog died she grieved, mourned, and lamented to the point that alarmed those around her. On the other hand, she seduced both Boy and Freddie taking more pleasure in doing that when one of the family was nearby. Once she detects a certain weakness in someone she hones in on those weaknesses at once. Good and evil coexisting and the struggle continues. "love and hate, sanity and insanity, death and birth … sin and redemption." Ibid., 769.

Sally Beauman later in her novel describes how Acland

married Jane Conyngham—the sole heiress of a large estate that bordered that of the Cavendish family. Acland and Jane had one daughter, Victoria. At her birth in January 1940 Constance came from America where she had been living with her husband Montague Stern. Acland had agreed that Constance should be one of Victoria's godmothers. Jane opposed the choice of Constance but her objection became open only the day before christening. It was too late by then.

At the church the baby was baptized; the sign of the cross was made. Constance wept. Two tears, then two more ran down from beneath the veil.

At the family gathering to celebrate Victoria's christening Constance had an argument with Maud—Denton's sister. The two ladies had some unfinished business. Before Constance got to marry Montague Stern he was involved with Maud who aspired to marry him some day. But Constance had made up her mind that she, not Maud, would marry Stern. And Constance won.

The dislike Constance had from Maud was not unfamiliar to Constance. As a defiant child she seemed always to expect such dislike from others.

The afternoon of the day of christening Constance went for a walk with Acland. She expressed her longing to see the old Stone House—Gwen's favorite place where she used to keep her watercolors and flower press. Acland accompanied Constance there.

At the Stone House Constance tried to seduce Acland who gently rebuffed her attempt. He reminded her that he is married, and she is married.

At Winterscombe a special dinner had been planned

to celebrate the christening. It was just a family dinner. Constance, however, could not pass the opportunity to do some harm.

Hurt them Constance said to herself. "Since she was a child … she was never to understand that to punish others is a poor way to ensure the punishment of the self …. In ensuring that she became an outcast, she was passing sentence on herself." Ibid., 745.

A long-time family friend, Wexton, a poet, was invited together with his devoted wife, Winnie. She had been reading his latest collection of poems that were dedicated to Acland and Jane. Winnie started to quote certain lines from memory. The poem was about love—the kind of love she felt for her husband.

Constance chimed in. In a clear voice she said 'you do know, Winnie, that the poem was written to a man?' Winnie's neck then cheeks blushed crimson. Constance went on "Wexton is describing love making, of course, … between two men. The kind Wexton prefers. The kind Stennie prefers too …. Steenie and Wexton used to be lovers." Ibid., 746.

Winnie left the dinner and Freddie followed.

Constance then turned the subject to Boy. All the time the family pretended that Boy killed himself after suffering from the war syndrome. Constance said it had nothing to do with the war but it was because Boy liked little girls. Freddie saw the photographs Boy took of her when she was twelve. Constance hinted that Boy went further than just pornographic pictures to actual intercourse.

When Steenie tried to dismiss what Constance was

saying she responded: 'Your mascara is running. You are about to burst into tears, as usual.'

Acland got angry hearing all these accusations against his brothers. He turned to Constance saying: 'Why not tell us about this afternoon? After all, that is what provoked all this, wasn't it?' She defended herself and tried to draw pity by claiming that she is the outsider as she has always been. Jane reminded Constance that Acland's family took her in, and Acland agreed to have her as godmother for their newborn. Constance responded that she resented charity and patronage.

Eventually Constance rose and started to walk about the room. "Whenever I came to Winterscombe, I begin to feel … oh, very wicked …. I look around me, at this splendid family—and I itch to blow it up … Five minutes in this house and I turn into the most ardent revolutionary." Ibid., 752.

After lashing out at everyone, Constance could not leave Acland unscathed. She let Jane know about Acland's son Edgar from Jenna whom he loved at the time. Edgar has been dead for a long time—so "I suppose it is easier to pretend he never existed, to continue to lie about him. After all, so long as we all go on assuming he was Jack Hennessy's child, we're safe." Ibid., 753.

Jane said: "Acland and I have been married for twelve years, Constance. Rather too long for secrets. Jenna once lost a child. I have lost two …. Whatever happened in the past, it doesn't cause division. Can you understand that? … we deal with this in our way … Constance why do you do this? … to use a dead child as a weapon … Why ask to be a godmother, and then do this? … Why go to such lengths to cause pain to others? … Boy, Freddie, Acland—I know you care for them, Constance, so why behave as if you hate them? … Steenie is your friend—and you have hurt him." Ibid., 754.

Constance responded "I love them. They are my brothers." Jane quietly said "Then why hurt them, Constance? All it does is isolate you. Can't you see that you hurt yourself, far more than you could ever hurt us?"

The Dark Angel couldn't stop. She told Jane "You know why Acland married you? For your money. Because I told him to." Jane's answer was poised "You gave my husband a good advice. For which we're both grateful." Ibid., 755.

Constance snapped. As usual her rage was sudden, and physical. She smashed the table. Knives, forks, plates crashed to the floor. She began to hurl glasses. In her right hand she grabbed the stem of a wine glass, with one pointed shards still attached. "You think people don't do that—they don't cut themselves up in other people's dining rooms? I will."

"All right." Acland said folding his arms. "We'll watch. Go right ahead … make sure it is an artery and not a vein."

Constance words were revealing. "The dead walk up and down in this house. I can smell them … Where is my father? … Isn't he here? … I thought he was here. I heard his voice." Ibid., 756.

Just as her rage started suddenly, it ended abruptly. The tension left her body. Her hand fell. She looked at Acland, Jane, and Wexton and said "I'll go to bed now. It's all right.

Don't worry. I'll leave in the morning. What a horrible mess. I'm so sorry."

The morning after the episode, Constance left for New York. Montague Stern had a separation agreement ready for Constance to sign. When she refused he threatened divorce with terms a great deal less favorable than those of the separation agreement. She begged Stern not to leave her. This didn't work, and Constance left.

Years went by. In England, Acland and Jane went to Europe to recruit some orphans for the orphanage Jane owned and operated. They apparently were at the wrong place at the wrong time. These were the months leading up to the Second World War. There were riots, street violence, and Nazi louts. Winfred Hunter-Coote, a family friend, telephoned from Europe and told about a "border incident, a case of mistaken identity which would, naturally, be investigated at the highest levels of the Reich." Ibid., 60. Records of the incident have been kept in Berlin but had since been destroyed.

A week later, Victoria was told that her mother and father were dead. No one could find out for certain how Acland and Jane died and why.

With the danger of war looming over the Continent and the U.K., Victoria would be safer in America to live with her godmother, Constance.

In the years prior to her travel to New York, Victoria never got all her questions about her godmother answered to her satisfaction. When Victoria finally met Constance it was as if two strangers seeing each other for the first time.

Constance was erased from the family after the episode at the night of Victoria's christening.

Victoria went to live with Constance when she was a child and remained in her care for more than twenty years. She brought her up. Vicky regarded Constance as a mother, mentor, an inspiration, a challenge, and a friend. Constance "radiated energy, as the many men who suffered at her hands could have told you. Danger was the essence of her charm." Ibid., 12.

Constance was forceful, but she was also vulnerable. Victoria grew up with Constance but never felt she understood her. "I admired her, loved her, was perplexed and sometimes shocked by her—but I never felt I knew her." Ibid., 13.

When Vicki went to live with Constance, the latter was thirty eight, well-known internal decorator secure in her reputation as a 'latter-day Circe' probably because of the men. Her hectic career left a trail of broken men. The damage she inflicted was confined to the male sex. If women were damaged, it was incidental and accidental harmed in the fallout of Constance main attack.

But Victoria didn't believe her uncle Steenie recollections about Constance. After all, Vicki loved Constance who had been unfailingly kind to her.

Constance taught Victoria the business and art of internal decoration. She introduced her to customers, and Vicky did work in several European countries.

Victoria got married to Frank in London. Constance had tried hard to stop this marriage and begged Vicki not to leave her alone. When this did not work, Constance took her life.

The news of Constance death reached Vicki and Frank three weeks later. The circumstances of her death remained unexplained and attributed, finally, to accident. That would have pleased Constance. She "succeeded in dying, as she had lived, amid speculation and puzzlement." Ibid., 773. Vicki was thirty eight when Constance departed, just as when Vicki went to live with Constance. Was it a coincidence? Or she was guided by the symmetry of numbers? They never found Constance body.

A tragic end to a troubled life. Constance was handled a poor hand. The lemonade she tried to do with her lemon turned out to be both sweet and sour.

Her relationships were, for the most part, destructive. The only fruitful relationship she had was with Victoria, her godchild. Even this connection was not perfect (she tried to stop and delay Vicky's marriage just out of selfishness).

Was Constance all evil? Probably not. She loved and cared for Victoria for more than twenty years. When her first dog, Floss, was killed she deeply mourned him for a long time. When her last dog, Bertie, died of old age she decided never to have another one. A kind heart that mingled with deep psychological wounds inflicted early on in her childhood by none other than her biological father.

In her journals Constance wrote about her father and how he repeatedly sexually abused her as a child. She lost her mother when she was only two-years old. She lost the source of true love each child naturally longs for.

She couldn't forget what her father used to call her a

few years after the sexual abuse stopped and she began to understand what he was doing to her. "Stupid Constance. Ugly Constance. Papa said she smelled nasty. He said she tasted sour. He said she was small, her fault she was bleeding. Stupid little bitch, he said, your hands are clumsy." Ibid., 767. He said she was an albatross, a great dead lump round his neck, weighing him down, choking him, the way the snare choked the rabbit. "When he said that, Constance thought, I will kill him." Ibid., 766.

Did she actually kill her father? Or was it Jack Hennessy? Or Denton who ordered traps to catch the interlopers? No one knew for certain who murdered Shawcross.

After the suicide of Constance, Victoria thought she knew why Constance had given her those journals. Vicky thought that if they were full of death, they were also full of life, and love. "Constance had tried to be evenhanded." Ibid., 769.

Was Constance odd in her yearning for love? Bertrand Arthur Russell, the atheist British philosopher, longed for love. At the end of his life he said that "his longing for love had governed his life ... Love is the longing of the human heart in the most majestic terms." Zacharias, Ibid., 71.

Both the heart and the mind come together to guide the human being to the Utmost being. The French philosopher Blaise Pascal envisioned "two tests for belief : the empirical test—that which is based on investigation— and the existential test—that which is based on personal experience." Zacharias, Ibid., 79. To put it differently: the mind and the heart—the empirical and the existential— have to be connected." Zacharias, Ibid., 82.

How marvelous is the human mind? It is capable of sorting and storing information, new and old, in an astonishingly selective process. It may forget yesterday but hold tight to some early events that become deeply ingrained to shape human's behavior and attitude.

In other words, it is memory that controls us. We may try to close that thought and close that life but it does not work like that.

Beauman eloquently addresses the subject.

> "We cannot forget. We are the stuff of memory: … all those details, sequences, episodes, which we all carry around with us in our heads and which we call the past—that is what we are. We may try to control it—as Constance did, …selecting an image here, an event there, turning our own past into ordered, linear, comprehensive narratives. … but the past resists this kind of tweaking. … It has a life all its own, …. It is as tough as a microbe, as adaptive as a virus, and just when we think we've composed it in a pattern that suits us just fine, it re-forms; it transmutes …. And if we ignore this … it sends up a subversive little message: Up comes an image, an event, we thought had been safely forgotten. Hey, says the memory, … what about this? Don't you remember that? … I had spent eight years trying to forget happiness. … I had not succeeded. How much harder for Constance then, who was trying to forget abuse." Ibid., 309.

The mind—this three-pound organ—is the "most complex

and orderly arrangement of matter in the universe." Isaac Asimov, IN THE GAME OF ENERGY & THERMODYNAMICS YOU CAN'T EVEN BREAK EVEN, Smithsonian Journal, June 1970, p. 10. Though it appears from this statement that Asimov was giving God a compliment, "he remained an avowed atheist until his death in 1992. MORE THAN MEETS THE EYE, Richard A. Swenson, M.D., Navpress, Colorado Springs, Colorado, 2000, p. 39.

If man, despite all of our new discoveries, is still unable to totally comprehend the mind, the Creator has given us some guidelines on how to "bring into captivity every thought to the obedience of Christ." II CORINTHIANS, 10: 5.

The battle between good and evil starts in the mind. An evil thought crosses the mind. If allowed to linger the mind will look for, and eventually find a justification to follow with the wrong seed. Dealing with the problem early on is the only way out. Arguing with the devil is a lost battle for man.

Fighting Satan on our own is not a viable suggestion. But we have the Holy Spirit (the third person of the Trinity) living within us and willing to help us defeat evil once we ask Him or help. The Holy Spirit lives within the believer but does not impose Himself on man. He just whispers, and it is up to man to listen and obey or to ignore His whisper.

Constance was not introduced to God's word. She didn't hear about His forgiveness. Had she experienced or heard about the love of God, her life could have been different. If someone had told her about the parable of the prodigal son, Constance could have come to her senses and turned her life around. In any case the DARK ANGEL is a novel and the author decides how the story ends.

Chapter 2

BRIEF ENCOUNTER BETWEEN TWO EXTRAORDINARY MINDS

Months after the end of the Second World War, Oxford philosopher Isaiah Berlin met the Russian poet Anna Akhmatova. They met in Leningrad to discuss literature in a private apartment. It was an unforgettable encounter, "a kind of intellectual and spiritual communion, as devoid of political content as it was chaste." Nial Ferguson, THE SQUARE AND THE TOWER. Penguin Press, New York, 2018, 246 – 53.

With Stalin in power such a meeting couldn't be overlooked. It was used as evidence to justify further persecution, and Akhmatova's life was nearly destroyed.

Akhmatova, born as Anna Andreevna Gorenko, was already an established poet before the 1917 Revolution. Her first husband, nationalist writer Nikolay Gumeliv, had been executed in 1921 for anti-Soviet sentiment and activity. This put Akhmatova under a cloud of suspicion.

Her fourth book of poetry was widely received causing a lot of consternation for the authorities. "Her work ceased to be published after 1925." Ibid., 246. In 1935 her son, Lev Gumeliv, and her third husband, Nikolai Punin, were both arrested.

Boris Pasternak, a friend of Akhmatova, advised her to write a letter to Stalin begging for the release of the only two people who are close to her. Surprisingly, Stalin agreed. He wrote on her letter an order that the two men be released. But Gumeliv was arrested again in March 1938 and sentenced to ten years in Arctic labor camp—the world's northernmost settlement.

Akhmatova was briefly rehabilitated in 1939. However, the publication of a selection of her poems brought a swift backlash. The head of the Leningrad Party ordered the seizure of the book condemning her lechery.

Between 1935 and 1940, Akhmatova wrote most of her poems about the terror which brought the agony to the millions who lost their loved ones to Stalin's heartless tyranny.

Isaiah Berlin had been born in Russia to a prosperous Jewish family in 1909. The Berlin's family had opted to leave the Soviet Union in 1920. A year later they settled in London. Well versed in the Russian language, he got a temporary posting as first secretary at the British embassy in Moscow in the summer of 1945.

On a visit to Leningrad Berlin met Akhmatova in a second-hand bookshop and they became acquainted with each other. Anna invited him to her apartment on November 14, 1945. A few days later Berlin paid a second visit to her place before his return to Moscow on the twentieth. During this meeting the "transformative connection occurred."

Berlin told her about friends who, like his family, had fled Russia after the Revolution. She talked about her childhood by the Black Sea, her marriages, her love for poet Osip Mandelstam who died in 1938 in the Gulag. They continued their literary discussion until late the next morning and it made an indelible impression on both of them.

Berlin's discussion with Akhmatova made him aware of "how completely the Soviet regime had destroyed the literary and artistic networks of pre-1920s Europe … [she] knew scarcely anything about the more recent work of writers and artists she had previously known." Ibid., 248. In fact, Berlin had been amazed to find that Anna is still living. He was only her second foreign visitor since the First World War.

Akhmatova's whole life was 'one of uninterrupted indictments of Russian reality,' Berlin observed. But she decided not to move—she was willing to die in her own country.

On January 5, 1946 the two had a brief meeting before Berlin's return to London. She gave him a volume of her earlier work. He thought her poetry is a work of genius. Their encounter had been behind his diversion from philosophy to the history of political thought where he did his best work in defense of individual freedom.

One commentator has written about Berlin and Akhmatova accidentally meeting each other: 'There was no physical contact. This must be one of the purest encounters between two human personalities on record. Two extraordinary minds seem for a moment to have engaged perfectly together to drive each other up to even greater heights of mutual love and understanding.'

Pasternak wrote to Berlin the following year telling him that Akhmatova developed something of an infatuation with Berlin.

For Akhmatova, her meetings with this foreigner were disastrous. During Berlin's first visit to Akhmatova it was incongruous to see the prime minister's son Randolph Churchill outside her apartment. Within days, the secret police had installed microphones in the ceiling of her home. Her peril worsened when she accepted an invitation to give a poetry reading in the House of Unions in Moscow. The audience's reception was ecstatic. Four months later in Leningrad the scene was repeated.

To draw such public attention didn't please the Soviet authorities. Surveillance of her and her friends intensified.

Akhmatova was publicly humiliated; her modest pension and food ration were only temporarily suspended. She stopped communicating with Berlin.

Her son, Lev—released from prison to fight in the ongoing war—was rearrested in 1949 and sentenced to a further ten years in a camp. Her third husband Punin was also rearrested and died in the Gulag.

The death of Stalin led to a slight thaw in the relationship with Britain. In 1956 Berlin returned to Russia but Akhmatova did not want to meet him for fear her son— newly released—should suffer.

In 1965, Akhmatova visited Oxford to receive an honorary degree. She assured Berlin that their meeting had angered Stalin so much that it 'started the Cold War and thereby changed the history of mankind.'

The meeting of minds—especially extraordinary minds

can do miracles. It can drive each other up to ever greater heights of mutual … understanding, and achievement. And it is not necessarily between a man and a woman as in the case of Berlin and Akhmatova. The same occurs when the brilliant graduate student is 'discovered' by his confident, secure professor who, over the years, becomes his guide and mentor.

CHAPTER 3

ORDINARY MINDS AND EXTRAORDINARY MINDS

Trained to be a scientist, it is not surprising for the author to find out that tackling a subject in the realm of psychology to be both interesting as well as challenging.

A career that extended for more than forty-five years spent mostly in the laboratory tends to shape the mind to deal with, and look for, concise, clear-cut, evident results. Chemical reactions are controlled qualitatively, and measured quantitatively. Not when dealing with a human being, and more so the human mind.

A miracle in its own right, the mind is one of the many blessings the Creator has bestowed on man. Compared with the other body organs it has the most complex, varied 'job description;' it observes, records, retrieves, arranges, and rearranges a continuous array of incoming scenes, data, information, about almost everything in the universe.

"Because of the variety of human beings who inhabit this earth [7.6 billion as of August 2018—a recent United Nations estimate], emanating from an enormous range of cultures, there are innumerable ways in which individuals can stand out and make a difference." Howard Gardner, EXTRAORDINARY MINDS, 1997, Basic Books, New York, 158.

Chiefly since the Enlightenment in the Seventeenth century, mankind enjoyed the luxury of allowing our talents and ideas to develop freely and fully in whichever ways they can.

To get a glimpse of the workings of the human mind, Sigmund Freud and Jean Piaget (the two most famous students of human development) focused on the child. This may not be surprising since we are born with the blueprint of our personality, behavior, and intelligence—as determined by our genes. Undoubtedly, as we get older our life experiences, environment, and dominant culture would diverse and play a very significant role in our adult contribution, or lack thereof, to humanity.

Freud (1856 – 1939) stressed the child's relationship to other human beings: the baby's relationship to his mother and siblings relationships with one another. A child growing up in a small family with one or no siblings at all would have different experiences from another with a number of brothers and sisters. The first does not have the urge to fight for an object—a toy—whereas the latter has to carve his/her niche in the family.

Whereas Sigmund Freud was interested in the individual's relationship to other human beings, Jean Piaget (1896 – 1980) was concerned with the child's cognitive development: the growth of intellectual powers. The central activity of the child's development is his/her relationship to the world of objects. Early on, these objects are tangible then as a youth s/he starts to deal with intangible entities.

On the spiritual side, renowned godly men such as the late Billy Graham, and the contemporary Dr. Charles Stanley told about dedicating their lives to God when they were still in their early youth years (the United Nations define youth range as 15 – 24). At that early age, both had the mental capacity to think of the Creator of the universe—the ultimate intangible deity confirming Piaget's hypotheses.

It is true many of Freud and Piaget specific claims have been challenged, but still current studies build on the approaches devised by the two.

Gardner states "the mind of the infant is already a quite detailed and articulated mental apparatus." Ibid., 19.

Almost from birth infants recognize their own mothers face and sound. By the end of the first year, most infants have established strong attachment bonds to the important people in their lives and when separated from them the infant become uneasy.

Infants can distinguish the world of persons from that of objects. Whereas infants engage in subtle exchanges with the beloved individuals around them, they have no similar reactions to toys or household objects. It is true the infant can develop a strong tie to a stuffed animal or a favorite pillow but such relations are simply an effort to 'infuse lifelike properties' into otherwise non responsive objects.

The symbols gradually enter the child's world. Symbols are a uniquely human phenomenon. The crafts as well as the disciplines of our adult world (the domains) are constructed on the basis of symbols.

Young children quickly learn to speak. First they know a few words when they are one-year old, then at three they can speak in simple sentences, and by the age of five they are quite articulate and are able to tell and appreciate simple stories and jokes.

Other symbol systems show growth as well. Response to music gets more refined as the child ages from one to five years. Ability to express himself by drawing develops from odd lines and dots on a page at the age of one to well-organized landscape at five or six years of age. Growth also occurs in other symbol systems such as dance, reading maps, and dealing with numbers.

It can safely be said that the five- or six-year-old has developed direct connection to the world of persons as well as that of objects.

Nevertheless, the mind still seems unformed. As the child begins school s/he starts to encounter scholarly disciplines. The passions of jealousy or pride are yet mostly unknown. It is difficult for the child to "think in terms of wide distances or long periods of time." Ibid., 24.

At the age of five, however, a few can advance cognitively on his/her own without much direct help from adults. A prodigy expresses his experiences with astonishing speed and precision.

The five-year old's world is flexible and imaginative. He can invent stories and draw objects the way he likes. To put it differently, the child follows his/her own genius.

Soon the child will be forever exposed to the practices

and beliefs of the dominant culture. How he interacts with the possibilities and constraints of the society will determine whether his natural predispositions would lead him to new heights—extra ordinariness.

The prevailing culture asserts itself forcefully in the years following early childhood after the child had already developed those capacities and skills that are preordained. The child's fate is tied to the options and the institutions that exist within that culture at the time.

Consider the case of two five-year olds of the same mental capacity with one born in an under developed country and the other in a developed, prosperous society.

The child born in a developed country will have the chance to benefit from all of the advantages available: good education, healthy clean environment, good nutrition, outdoor sports, and a variety of gadgets and toys. All these factors enhance and help develop his/her innate capacities and skills. The door to achieving new heights is open.

Howard Gardner, a Harvard professor, looks at the mastery of skills, and how some individuals gain skills more rapidly than others. He attributes the phenomenon to more general intelligence, special intelligence in some domain, high motivation, or the availability of better instructors.

Scientists working on quantifying expertise say that it takes about ten years of serious practice to become an expert. Cognitivists believe that any person who applies himself for several years could attain the status of full-fledged expert. Only practice separates the ordinary from the extraordinary.

Schools are the institutions charged with training

students on how to employ the notations of their culture: written language and numerical systems. Historically, however, the mission of schools has changed to suit the demands of society.

In the nineteenth century, college-bound students had to learn two or more classical languages. In the twentieth century, college-bound students have to study higher mathematics and modern foreign languages and perform well on standardized multiple-choice tests.

The fact remains, however, that "rarely are these behaviors actually required for success in the broader society. Rather, … they serve as a proxy for higher achievement." Ibid., 29.

A case in point. The author eldest daughter scored above average in the SAT. She got a degree in Chemical Engineering with high GPA that put her in Medical School. She has been practicing medicine in a big city for more than fifteen years. Her sister also scored average on the SAT then got her Chemical Engineering degree with 3.0 GPA. More and more, standardized multiple-choice tests are proving non indicative of success in higher education. Safwat Bishara and Dawlat Bishara, ABOUT LEARNING AND EDUCATION. A PARENT AND EDUCATOR'S VIEW SUPPORTED BY OVERSEAS EXPERIENCE, Authorhouse, Bloomington, IN, 2015.

It must be pointed out that achieving scholarly or disciplinary high grades, that is success, is not the same as achieving extraordinariness. By the same token, expertise is not extraordinariness.

To achieve extraordinariness the bright, talented

individual must posses the desire and ambition for greatness, and be living in a society that provides the means for producing and encouraging innovative performers.

No one can deny that there are differences between human beings. Differences can be tangible: facial features, finger prints, hair and dental imprints are used to differentiate between the 7.6 billion people. Differences are also intangible. Individuals differ in skills, habits, beliefs, and aspirations.

Whereas no scientist denies the differences among human beings, they differ on the significance of these differences. Some think that "these differences are not that important or that, while important, they take a backseat to the determination of human universals." Ibid., 31.

Since infancy the differences can be observed.

1. The temperament shows itself clearly. Some are quiet and passive while others are active, energetic, and resist stress.

2. Young children develop at different speeds. Some speak or understand better than others, some are able to remember more accurately at an early age, and some score higher on the early versions of intelligence tests.

3. Children differ also in their personalities. Some have self-confidence, self-restraint, and willingness to take risks. How they value companionship, independence, or competition varies from one child to the other.

4. More crucially, they differ in their characteristic intellectual strengths. Some show proclivities in their languages, but not in their music or spatial abilities. Some children manifest an early spurt in their drawings

but not in their dealing with numbers, or their ability to relate to and discern motivations of others.

One of the marvels of creation is to notice the wide spectrum within the areas of relative strength, and the areas of discernible weakness, between the worldwide billions of human beings. We share a few features such as having two hands, two legs, two eyes, two ears, and one nose but differ in everything else being tangible or intangible.

CHAPTER 4

DEVELOPMENT OF EXTRAORDINRY MINDS

Some humans are bright. They are extraordinary—a special class of individuals.

But the question is: What is the source of their unusual psychometric intelligence?

Most experts agree that intelligence is hereditary with the biological parents as the most influential entities. Genes are a more powerful contributor to measured intelligence than does environment.

But then, will children who are psycho-metrically bright be good at learning all disciplines, or will they do better in some and less so in others?

For almost a hundred years, the IQ tests were applied to quantitatively measure children's ability to learn. Those with high IQ are good at learning what is featured at school. But here is the caveat. If the intelligence test involves much "decoding of linguistic and numerical notational systems, it will predict quite accurately how children will do in the standard subjects in school. If, on the other hand, the test relies on non-notational skills (like solving mazes), or if the school environment … focuses on projects rather than on short-answer written tests, then … psychometric intelligence will less accurately predict student's performance in school." Howard Gardner, EXTRAORDINARY MINDS, Basic Books, 1997, 40, 41.

The viewpoint Gardner raises about intelligence is radically different from the standard view endorsed by psychologists and laypersons. It has been thought that intelligence is simple entity often dubbed "g" for general intelligence.

How intelligent you are is almost wholly determined by your biological parents, and there is not much one can do to change his/her inborn intelligence. The measurement of intelligence has also developed over time. At first, psychologists used clinical interviews or pencil and paper measurements; now intelligence can be approximated through analysis of patterns of brain waves or measurement of the time it takes a person to react to two flashes of light.

Gardner reports that information gathered over the past century from biology, psychology, and anthropology "directly contradicts the key claims of the standard view." Ibid., 35. Biology informs us that it is practically impossible to isolate genetic from environmental factors. We simply can not design the crucial experiments.

Psychology tells that humans possess many different intellectual areas that are considerably independent from one another. Again it is futile to try to separate a unitary intelligence from the rest due to problems associated with measurements.

From anthropology we have learned that culture contributes immensely to learning and motivation. South Korean and Japanese students score at the top on international tests such as the Program for International Student Assessment (PISA). Amanda Ripley, THE SMARTEST KIDS IN THE WORLD AND HOW THEY GOT THAT WAY. Simon and Schuster, New York, London, Toronto, Sydney, New Delhi, 2013. Ripley describes how those societies stress hard work and set high expectations for their school children.

The same features that Ripley describes as dominant in some Asian countries apply for some Middle Eastern countries such as Egypt, Syria, Lebanon, and Jordan. Great emphasis is put on education as the path for a better life.

MULTIPLE INTELLIGENCES

Gardner has developed his theory of Multiple Intelligences (MI) in the 1980s. It is based on "knowledge of the development of the brain; findings obtained from special populations (… autistic individuals and prodigies); and identification of abilities and skills that are esteemed in cultures very different from our own." Howard Gardner, Ibid., 35.

The list of distinct forms of intelligence included
1. Linguistic intelligence
2. Logical intelligence (these two types are central in schools and school examinations)
3. Spatial intelligence (dealing effectively with large spaces and/or spatial layouts)

4. Musical intelligence (ability to create and perceive musical patterns)
5. Body kinesthetic intelligence (capacity to solve problems or create products using the whole, or parts of the body)
6. Personal Intelligence (dealing with, and understanding of, other persons)
7. Personal intelligence oriented toward understanding of oneself
8. Natural world intelligence exhibited by hunters and botanists who have the apprehension of the natural world (this form of intelligence has been added by Gardner in the 1990s).

To be sure, we all have the full range of intelligences but to different degrees. Individuals differ in their respective strengths and weaknesses. The Creator in His wisdom bestowed a gift on every human being. Different talents enrich the society and help satisfy the needs of everyone.

By the same token, a few are particularly gifted and distinguish themselves as extraordinary or exceptionally bright. We must distinguish between the "typically bright" and the "exceptionally bright."

In 1925, Lewis Terman published a study of 1500 high-IQ children growing up in California. The Terman sample is considered "the best-studied in the world, for the subjects have been followed from childhood until the present, when the survivors are generally in their eighties." Gardner, Ibid., 38. Those typically bright individuals did well according to any measure: they enjoyed good health, reasonable wealth, a sense of accomplishment and content with their lives.

The typically bright can read before school age. They listen to books that are red to them by adults, memorize the texts, then try to link the visual patterns and the words. By the age of three or four, they can read fluently, and by the time they reach school they may well be able to read books at the level of middle-school children and discuss their contents in a detailed manner.

But the relationship between early reading ability and high psychometric intelligence is not essential. There are early readers who are not otherwise bright, and there are high-testers who read at the normal age or are even delayed at the onset of the learning process.

Our conception of scholarly intelligence is wholly tied to the ability to master arbitrary notations (letters) and to use them speedily. But dealing with print is but one facet of intelligence. (Albert Einestein was a poor student in his first years of school.)

THE EXCEPTIONALLY BRIGHT

Impressive as they are, the typically bright lacked creative accomplishments. Few, if any, came to be featured as creative artists or writers, or scientists of Nobel-prize caliber.

As early as 1942, the educational psychologist Leta Hollingworth looked at some unusual students—those that fell in the category of one in a hundred thousand, rather than one in a thousand. Children with an IQ over 180 are an unhappy group. They are so different from their age mates to find things in common; as misfits they are prone to anxieties and to severe social and emotional problems. Such children function well socially when placed with others who are their intellectual equals regardless of their age.

Ellen Winner's book GIFTED CHILDREN, 1966, reported on some features of the "exceptionally bright." They possess notable energy, curiosity, and focus on domains that interest them. The exceptionally bright are persistent learners; it is often hard to take them away from their areas of passion. They are self-propelled, set their own schedule, and do not welcome their parents telling them to study.

Most scholars agree with Dr. Samuel Johnson that true genius is "a mind of large general powers, accidentally determined to some particular direction." W. J. Bate, SAMUEL JOHNSON, Harvest, New York, 1975, 252. The idea is that if you are good at one thing, you could be good at almost anything.

There are those, however, who believe that students who excel in school may be unsuccessful outside of school, just as individuals who couldn't perform well in school turn out to be very successful in business or in the arts. Moreover, there are populations that are notably good at one thing, such as idiot savants, or notably poor at one thing just like children with selective learning disabilities. These observations stand in contrast to the view that intelligence is "a single entity, under the operation of a single machine, that functions either well or poorly across the board." Gardner, Ibid., 41.

Generalizations do not bode well when it comes to human beings. Both views concerning intelligence and success are represented in real life. There are those who are able to learn most things with equal ease. Many students are quite able to do well across a wide range of school disciplines and continue to be successful in real life after schooling. There are also those who present uneven profiles in school. They may be very good in linguistics but have serious difficulties in science or mathematics. Some individuals have an excellent engineering mind but have difficulty in composing a coherent paragraph. And there are those who were indifferent students but became exceptional leaders, such as Winston S. Churchill, or renowned inventors, such as Thomas Alva Edison.

To sum it up, Gardner says

> "pay one's respect to school and IQ tests, but do not let them dictate one's judgment about an individual's worth or potential. ... what is important is an individual's actual achievements in the realms of work and personal life." Ibid., 42.

In the subject of extraordinary minds, a fundamental question is the role of culture and experience. In other words, are the outstanding accomplishments of exceptionally bright people the result of intellectual powers the child is born with or that the dominant culture is a contributing factor?

In Western societies, the standard psychometric theory is widely adopted. It credits accomplishments largely to the intellectual powers the child brings to any learning situation. Most parents are reluctant to interfere with the child's intellectual growth during the first years of life.

On the other hand, societies influenced by Confucian ideas, like Japan and China, minimize the significance of inborn intelligence. Accomplishments are primarily a function of motivation, hard work, ability to learn from errors, and the teacher or coach's skill and qualification. Both the parents and teachers strive to develop habits of order, discipline, and respect for the elders in the preschool years.

Growing up in Egypt, the author(s) recalls a culture that stresses respect of those who are older than you. One can learn valuable lessons from those who had experienced life longer. Life experiences may or may not be directly related to intelligence, but they certainly entail wisdom. In a culture that extends seven thousand years, youngsters have a trough of actual stories treasured from one generation to the next.

ACTS, 7: 22 says "And Moses was learned in all the wisdom of the Egyptians, and was mighty in words and in deeds."

Moses died in 1407 B.C., that is, he lived during the fourteenth century B.C. Going back 3500 years, the Egyptian culture was already advanced, civilized, and welcoming as the Bible tells us.

A question here poses itself: Is wisdom a form of intelligence? Gardner lists wisdom as one of the higher-level cognitive processes such as common sense, originality, and metaphorical ability, see Chapter 13. It might be difficult to measure wisdom just as it is difficult to measure personal intelligence that deals with understanding other people or understanding oneself.

In the development of extraordinary minds, the debate continues on the relative importance of 'talent' and 'training.' Psychologist Anders Ericsson and his colleagues provided a lot of evidence that in the domains of memorization of digits or musical performance the number of deliberate practice hours make all the difference to differentiate skilled practitioners from one another. Ericsson, however, did not address the role of talent.

Others, including Gardner, believe that sheer practice is just not enough to be affective in highly cognitive domains such as mathematics and musical composition. Besides, only those with talent are likely to practice for thousands of hours. Absent talent, the incentive to practice reverses to boredom.

Talent coupled with practice seem to be the binary ingredients that lead to outstanding accomplishments. Talent without long hours of persistent practice would be a waste, and mere practice without in borne talent is unlikely to continue or to yield results. To put it differently, precocity shows itself if an individual has a high psychometric intelligence, or a special gift in some other kind of intelligence, *and* strong support from family and the surrounding culture.

Unusual levels of performance by five-year old prodigies can come from two different groups: i- children of high psychometric intelligence, and ii- children who may be less remarkable but are fortunate to be exposed to a good teaching method that either develops specific skills

(Suzuki method for playing violin) or provides a rich set of experiences (cultivation of crafts at the Reggio Emilia schools).

Early or premature development has been observed in three domains: chess, musical performance, and mathematical understanding. Some believe that these three forms precocity are related to a central talent with numerical or spatial patterns. This hypotheses fits the view of a general intellect.

But the fact is that "most youngsters are precocious in one of these domains, not all three; and that while there is a numerical component to each, spatial abilities are far more important in chess, [while] musical sensitivity and physical dexterity are of essence in musical performance." Gardner, Ibid., 45. This seems to support the theory of multiple intelligences.

A challenging group to psychologists are those individuals who are extremely impaired in most domains, except a single one. These children are often autistic, that is, their communicative capacities in any symbol system fall in between very weak and nonexistent.

John and Michael, a pair of autistic twins, were able to calculate large sums and to identify the day of the week of any date from the nineteenth century. Leslie Lemke was blind and retarded but taught himself how to play the piano with great skill, most of the time learning complex pieces after a single hearing.

The above, and other, cases of autism are but some evidence of the marvels of the human mind. We still have a lot to discover about this three-pound organ.

Autistic people possess a single preserved intellectual capacity that reflects an intelligence, or a set of intelligences, that focus with astonishing accuracy on a domain to which the child has been exposed. Experts believe that autistic individuals are exceptional in certain domains simply because they are not bothered about how to express themselves or communicate with others.

It is imperative to note that ultimate achievements may not always be evident early in life. Some individuals are late bloomers: Charles Darwin was an indifferent student, and Harry Truman was a certified failure at age forty." Ibid., 48.

Skill in some domains may not emerge until adolescence or sometimes later. Some ordinary people may be catapulted to great accomplishments as a result of the intervention of circumstances whether encouraging or bitter.

CHAPTER 5

TYPES OF EXTRAORDINARINESS

Three distinct features characterize extraordinary people. First, the practices of the domain that they master maybe varied in a significant way, or they attempt to overthrow these practices altogether. Second, individuals with extraordinary minds make a conscience decision whether to focus on the realm of human beings (persons), or on objects. That is, they have interest in the domains of knowledge that "exist in one's society … [or] in the human beings who populate the society." Gardner, Ibid., 125. Virginia Woolf and Winston Churchill were extraordinary; Woolf turned inward to herself whereas Churchill was a great influencer. Freud and Einstein were students of the science of psychology and mathematics, respectively.

The third feature that characterize extraordinary people is whether creativity exists solely inside the head of the creative individual, or it emerges from the interaction among three elements: the person with the talent, the domain of work, and the judgments wrought by the surrounding judges.

Needless to say, these distinctions are not clear cut. Almost all extraordinary persons exhibit more than one form of excellence. And most extraordinary individuals also have weaknesses. Freud was a master of physical science but poor in mathematics. His domain of excellence (objects) also required knowledge about human beings.

However, there are several additional forms of extraordinariness that help identify the unusual and notable.

An individual may be able to get the attention of people involved in a particular field or the larger society and become famous. There is no requirement for a talent or a need for a contribution to a domain.

Success and fame are close but not exactly identical. Success usually implies the acquisition of material resources through persistent hard work. An individual who makes a contribution to a domain achieves success.

Whereas fame or celebrity does not exclude real creativity it can not be confused with it. A creative person must change a domain; a celebrity is a person who is famous for being famous—actors and actresses are some examples.

Some individuals influence others by the originality of their work. But another form of influence can be exerted by people whose very presence is enough to affect those who come into contact with them. Gardner calls this spiritual extraordinariness. Pope John XXIII, Mahatma Ghandi, Mother Teresa, and Martin Luther King, Jr. could stimulate others to alter their consciousness to the better.

Unfortunately, the power to influence others could be devious. Cult leaders like David Koresh and Reverend Jimmy Jones, as well as nationalist leaders like Adolf Hitler,

Gamal Abd El Nasser, and Mao Zedong exerted a spiritual hold over many trusting, believing followers.

Those with such power over others share some common features. They often have striking physical appearance that exudes charm and energy that is coupled with hypnotic powers. This helps convince listeners that they are addressed directly and singularly. Influencers (gurus) are extremely knowledgeable about the art of manipulation of others. They aspire to "suppress the 'enthusiast's' own individuality by merging it with the consciousness of the omniscient spiritual figure." Gardner, Ibid., 130.

Positive spiritual hegemony over others always involves a message or idea. But for the guru, the ideas are not primary—they are mere conduits for seducing others.

Some individuals have the knowledge of self or others, interests in a domain of knowledge or skill, who can harness their abilities to a broader concern: the improvement of life conditions for those other than themselves. They earn the descriptor of spiritual extraordinary. They believe passionately in what they are doing, and they are overwhelmingly positive in attitude. Their beliefs are often founded on religious basis. Good Samaritan (Franklin Graham) and Covenant House are but some examples.

Gardner points out that the capacity to behave in a caring way is separate from the capacity to reason effectively about moral dilemmas. These individuals can hardly be considered creative because they rarely thought of novel ways of helping others.

A distinct type of extraordinary people are those who stand out because of differences or deficiencies. The "combination of powers *and* deficits sometimes turns out to be productive." Ibid., 133. The Apostle Paul who wrote about two thirds of the NEW TESTAMENT endured some kind of physical impairment. He prayed to God to cure him of his ailment but the Lord responded "My grace is sufficient."

Obviously, the possession of defects does not in itself assure extraordinariness. Ludwig van Beethoven (December 1770 – March 1827) became deaf at a later stage of his life. He wasn't able to hear some of his best pieces put together later in his caree.

In Egypt, a Nobel prize candidate in literature was blinded at an early age as an infant when his mother mistakenly used iodine solution instead of eye drops. Taha Hussein grew up blind, went to school, then to college where he graduated at the very top of his class, went to the Sorbonne University to get his doctorate. Back in Cairo, he was appointed a faculty staff member, promoted to professorship then Dean of the College of Arts, Cairo University. His writings acquired him the honorary title: 'Dean of Arabic Literature.' His books were best sellers over the whole region, and some were produced as successful movies. Dr. Hussein achieved greatness while being blind. He was nominated more than once for the Nobel prize but the political environment at the time was unfavorable. His blindness probably helped him focus his attention for many hours at a time. Distractions were nonexistent.

Virginia Woolf was initially wounded, and eventually defeated, by an accumulation of traumas. The wounds did not deter, but probably enhanced, her attaining the extraordinary status.

Gardner notes that "a deficit in one cognitive or affective area may go hand-in-hand with the capacity to develop other kinds of strengths." Ibid., 135.

God is fair. A difficulty may turn out to be an opportunity depending on the individual involved. Instead of feeling victim, a strong-willed person may see an opportunity to be a victor.

On the other hand, some extraordinary people may excel in a number of unrelated domains. "500 years after his death, Leonardo's da Vinci's stunning creativity and foresight in science, the arts, and engineering continue to amaze us." Leonardo's Enduring Brilliance, by Claudia Kalb, NATIONAL GEOGRAPHIC, May 2019, 56 – 93. Windsor Castle has the Queen's collection of his *drawings.* As an *anatomist,* he dissected animal and human cadavers. As a *scientist,* he observed and documented the natural world in his notebooks. He lacked tools to demonstrate his idea that air and water share properties. As an *engineer,* he devised plans for bridges, buildings, and military equipment. He yearned to design a flying machine for humans. As an *inventor,* he wrote in his notebooks about an apparatus to allow divers to breath under water. As a *musician,* he researched acoustics, sang, and improvised melodies. He also deigned a range of musical instruments. As a *cartographer,* he designed maps for civil and military purposes.

Extraordinary individuals have the capacity to focus their attention for long periods of time planning their political or religious campaigns or creating works of science or art. Such attention, though desirable, is akin to autism—a condition in which the individual's attention is so focused that s/he is unable to engage in day-to-day human communication. It may not be surprising, then, that the incidence of autism is more prevalent in families who perform at high levels of science, mathematics, and engineering.

Gardner's studies about extraordinary individuals have two characteristics. First, the research is time- and culture-bound. It is focused on the modern era and to Western culture. Second, he applied no moral litmus test in deciding which individuals are extraordinary people who left marks on the persons and domains of their time. Gandhi's behavior towards his family, and Freud's treatment of his associates (and sometimes his data) did not preclude Gardner from including them as extraordinary.

The satisfaction of being extraordinary comes at a price—usually a high price.

To be sure, there are rewards for extraordinariness. Extraordinary individuals are treated as if they were important; they come to feel that they have made a difference during their lifetimes and possibly for the future. While this is true, there is a considerable cost to be paid.

First, it takes at least ten years of persistent involvement to master a domain, and thereafter the extensive work must continue.

Second, the extraordinary person is dangerously at risk for loneliness, pain, and rejection. "Most innovators and most innovations are not well understood or appreciated at the time of their launching." Ibid., 141. It is the nature of man, and the society at large, to be conservative, resistant to change. Peers are jealous, and the general public may not be receptive to new ideas.

Most extraordinary individuals are very difficult people—often tortured, inflicting suffering on those close to them. They are usually unhappy, liable to breakdowns, to feel suicidal, and to become estranged from close associates. A British newspaper ran the headline EINSTEIN = GENIUS MINUS NICENESS.

It is however, important to stress that extraordinary individuals are also capable of great acts of kindness and generosity. They may be brutal at times, but may well be noble persons at other times.

The appearance of savagery may simply be due to the intelligence differential that separates the extraordinary person from the majority of those around him/her. The speed and depth of the intellectual processing of information and data by the extraordinary-gifted person may be a source of frustration when dealing with the ordinary individuals.

Creativity or leadership can not be taught in a weekend workshop. It takes years, even decades, of consistent experience for the extraordinary career to unfold. The young prodigy would benefit to have adults who believe in the importance of steady effort to improve one's skills in a domain. Love and all kinds of support by role models are crucial. Parents or coaches are indispensable to help the youngsters to deal with the inevitable disappointments and setbacks.

Three interrelated features are regularly associated with extraordinary accomplishments.

First, Reflecting. It encompasses regular, conscious consideration of daily-life events viewed in the light of longer-term aspirations. The regular habit of thinking about what has happened to us and what it means keeps the mind focused on the preferred domain.

Reflecting may be achieved through written accounts of conversations to reflect on virtually every aspect of existence was Virginia Woolf's mode of reflecting. Gandhi took daily walks, meditated on a daily basis, and engaged in regular strategy sessions with his closest associates.

Second, Leveraging. Extraordinary individuals have the inherent capacity to ignore areas of weakness and concentrate instead on their own strengths to gain a competitive advantage in the domain in which they chose to work.

Freud was a Jew seeking recognition in anti-Semitic Vienna; Woolf had no formal education but was writing a new chapter in English literature. Because she was fragile in the face of criticism, she avoided face-to-face public debates and relied on written words to meet others on her strongest ground.

Stephen J. Gould, the admired scientist and writer, has weakness in the areas of mathematics or logic. He writes: "All people have oddly hypertrophied skills but some folks never identify their uniqueness properly …. I cannot forget or expunge any item that enters my head, and I can always find legitimate and unforced connections among the disparate details." Gould, 1995, xi-xii.

People with extraordinary minds can think about a given problem in a number of ways, particularly ways that have not previously been brought to bear on that problem.

Third, Framing. It is "the capacity to identify one's own deviance and to convert it into a competitive advantage." Gardner, Ibid., 149. In other words, framing involves the ability to construe experiences in a positive way, in a way that allows the person to draw germane lessons that helps re-energize him/her. Critical is the capacity to find meaning—and even uplift—in an apparently negative experience and to apply it as fuel to face life confidently and effectively. A setback is an event others might deem an experience to be quickly forgotten, but it benefits the extraordinary individual who reflects on it, work it over, and discern which aspects might harbor avenues about how to avoid repeating in the future.

Extraordinary individuals, by definition, have an impact on the lives of many people extending in most cases to cover the globe. The change they bring is not restricted to one lifespan but usually lasts for centuries. It is therefore desirable, if not imperative, for extraordinariness to be humane.

Gardner puts it this way

> "Because of the variety of human beings who inhabit this earth, emanating from an enormous range of cultures, there are innumerable ways in which individuals can stand out and make a difference." Ibid., 158.

Mainly in the West and chiefly since the Enlightenment we enjoy the luxury of allowing our talents to develop freely in whichever ways they may go.

But, the risk of destroying or radically remaking our

world looms large. And here we are confronted with an epochal dilemma. If we allow the Maker (one who have mastered existing domains but devotes energies to create a new domain) and the Influencer (the person whose primary goal is the influencing of other individuals) to express themselves freely, without regard for the consequences, we risk destroying our world (say by a new weapon) or rendering our world uninhabitable (by a genetic experiment that has run out of control).

If, on the other hand, we enact severe measures to limit such expression, we renounce the very liberties for which many people have worked honestly over the centuries.

Humane creativity or humane extraordinariness entails that "with the invaluable opportunity to use one's mind and resources freely, there should come a concomitant responsibility to use them well and humanely." Ibid., 159.

We as society cannot impute responsibility for the uses of our words, our works, our inventions to religions, courts of law, or some other community. Rather, this vigilance should be the responsibility of the individuals who are blessed with the opportunity of initiating new lines of creation.

In reality, the seeds for humane extraordinariness do exist. The artistic and professional domains have guiding principles that illustrate the phenomenon. Consider the "Hippocratic oath for doctors, the truthfulness of the scholar, the dedication to justice of the lawyer, the disinterestedness of the guardian" all address man's conscious to do the right thing.

Looking closely one realizes that *all* seeds of humane

behavior are found in the Word of God. MICAH, 6: 8 says He hath shewed thee, O man, what is good; and what doth the LORD require of thee, but to do justly, and to love mercy, and to walk humbly with thy God?

But these beliefs and practices have been blurred in recent years, because of carefully crafted powerful messages about self-interest and the marketplace.

CHAPTER 6

ORDINARY IS THE MAJORITY

The previous two chapters have dealt with the extraordinary minds. Individuals of this caliber leave an impeccable heritage to humanity. Nevertheless, they are the exception rather than the rule. Most of us are ordinary people. Surely, there is a wide spectrum that characterizes one individual from the other.

A fundamental question that faces every human being, during a certain stage of life or the other, is "How intelligent are you?" Each one of us is keen to know how smart he or she is. Parents are eager to find out how intelligent their offspring is. Teachers, either through personal observation during class or through standardized tests, form their ideas about how each student ranks on the scale of smartness.

For more than a hundred years, the IQ test did exert a powerful hold on the imaginations of millions of Americans. Quantification of a phenomenon is always desirable as it provides a quantitative measure of the criteria. The IQ test provides a numerical value of smartness that allows grown-ups to categorize children with potential for success. Those who score high are considered gifted or genius (IQ score of 140 or more).

By the same token, those who score at the low end of the IQ test are labeled retarded. Worse yet, words such as moron, idiot, and imbecile were, at one time, regarded as scientifically correct ways of describing low scorers.

Over the years, however, evidence and research have shown that the IQ test is tilted toward measuring but two types of intelligence: the linguistic and the logical-mathematical. They provide a good prediction of the scholarly achievements during school years, but not much about success in real life after school.

The theory of Multiple Intelligence (MI) shows that there are many ways to be smart. Intelligence is not restricted to the linguistic (verbal) and the logical-mathematical areas. Each one of us has multiple talents.

In 1983, Dr. Howard Gardner published his book FRAMES OF THE MIND: THE THEORY OF MULTIPLE INTELLIGENCES. Basic Books. He theorized that there are seven kinds of smart. These are: linguistic, logical-mathematical, spatial, bodily-kinesthetic, musical, interpersonal, and intrapersonal.

Dr. Thomas Armstrong, in his book 7 KINDS OF SMART, Penguin Putnam Inc., New York, N.Y., 1999, 241 explained that for an intelligence type to be qualified as such it has to fulfill all of eight criteria.

1. Potential Isolation By Brain Damage.

As neuropsychologist and professor of neurology at Boston University School of Medicine, Gardner came to understand that "brain injuries or illness were oftentimes selective with respect to intelligences. That is, an individual could have a lesion in one area of the brain which might devastate a particular intelligence while leaving other cognitive faculties alone."

In his book THE SHATTERED MIND, Dr. Gardner writes about the French composer Maurice Ravel. Hit by a stroke in his seventies devastated his ability to speak and write. But he was still able to perform and critique music—abilities that were in other areas of the brain that must have been unaffected by the ravages of the stroke.

Armstrong lists names of the specific areas of the brain that seem to be related to each type of intelligence. Armstrong, Ibid., 242.

2. THE EXISTENCE OF IDIOTS SAVANTS, PRODIGIES, AND OTHER EXCEPTIONAL INDIVIDUALS.

Savants are individuals who are excellent in one particular intelligence but who, for the most part, have significant difficulties with the others.

The Oscar-winning movie RAIN MAN, based on a true story, is about a man named Raymond. He is an autistic who had a phenomenal ability to calculate numbers despite having poor social skills (interpersonal intelligence), undeveloped language ability (linguistic intelligence), and a diminished sense of self (intrapersonal intelligence). Despite his severely underdeveloped intelligence in the linguistic, interpersonal, and intrapersonal skills, Raymond has highly developed logical-mathematical intelligence.

The above case is by no means an anomaly. There are

many other cases of autistic individuals. An autistic young man was reported to have the ability to memorize the names and numbers of individuals listed in the phone directory (prior to the introduction of smart phones).

The existence of people with such disparaging skills may be a proof that intelligences exist autonomously from each other; one specific intelligence can develop to an extraordinary level, while the other intelligences are left far behind.

Could this be some sort of a Heavenly justice? The lack in some types of intelligence is compensated by an extraordinary abundance in one other type of intelligence? Just like those who have lost their eye sight whereas their hearing senses get so sharp as a means to help them compensate for the lost sight.

Armstrong, Ibid., 244 – 5, provides some examples of people who have a well developed type of intelligence but lack in other types.

a. Linguistic: Low IQ individuals who can read encyclopedias but without comprehension.

b. Logical-Mathematical: People with low IQ who can memorize train tables, or tell the day of the week your birthday will fall in the year 3000.

c. Spatial: Autistic persons who have outstanding drawing abilities such as a five-year-old girl who had gifted artistic abilities despite being labeled autistic.

d. Bodily-Kinesthetic: Autistic individuals who can physically mimic objects.

e. Musical: Some people with Williams syndrome have strong musical talents but has difficulty doing simple math. Gloria Lenhoff can sing opera in 26 different languages including Chinese but has no appetite for numbers.

f. Interpersonal: Some individuals have an uncanny ability to pin point nonverbal social cues even though they may be described as schizophrenic.

g. Intrapersonal: Individuals may have a highly developed sense of self but fail to communicate it to other people.

3. AN IDENTIFIABLE CORE OPERATION.

Each type of intelligence should have specific mechanisms, that is, core operations, for receiving information from the outer world and processing it just as a computer deals with an incoming set of data. (Actually, computers try to imitate the workings of the human mind, and not the other way around.)

The following are the critical operations identified by Gardner for each type of intelligence.

a. Linguistic: A sensitivity to the sounds, structures and meanings of words.

b. Logical-Mathematical: Capacity to pin point logical or numerical patterns. It has been said that numbers 'speak.'

c. Spatial: The ability to perceive the visual-spatial world accurately and in detail. Also to perform transformations on one's initial impressions.

d. Bodily-Kinesthetic: Capacity to control one's body movements and the skill to handle objects.

e. Musical: Appreciation of the forms of musical expressiveness, and ability to produce rhythm and pitch.

f. Interpersonal: Capacity to discern the moods, temperaments, motivations, and desires of others. And respond appropriately.

g. Intrapersonal: Ability to know one's own strengths and weaknesses to support the former and to avoid the latter. To be able to discriminate among one's emotions.

4. A DISTINCTIVE DEVELOPMENTAL HISTORY.

Dr. Gardner sought to integrate concepts of developmental psychology into the theory of multiple intelligences. He specified that "roles within each intelligence should have their own patterns of development, ranging from novice to expert." Armstrong, Ibid., 248.

Whereas specific universal stages might be identified for each intelligence type through which all must go through, yet there is room for tremendous individual variations

5. AN EVOLUTIONARY HISTORY.

According to Howard Gardner, for an intelligence to be included as a type of intelligence there must be evidence for it in the prehistoric life of humanity as well as in earlier stages of evolution, that is, in other species.

Gardner cites written notations dating to 3000 years ago; systems and calendars found in prehistoric settings; prehistoric tool use; musical instruments extending back to the Stone Age; cave drawings; and evidence of early communal living groups.

6. SUPPORT FROM EXPERIMENTAL PSYCHOLOGICAL TASKS.

Psychological experiments can help distinguish the different types of intelligences. Gardner suggests using those tasks that have to do with attention, memory, perception, and transfer to figure out the strengths (or weaknesses) of individuals.

Experiments might show that a person has a great memory for faces but not for words or numbers. (The author has a good memory for numbers but not for names which can sometimes be socially awkward.) Some tasks might reveal an individual's ability to learn mathematical concepts but this does not mean s/he is a good reader. That is, logical-mathematical intelligence does not necessarily transfer to linguistic intelligence. A tennis-playing ability does not transfer to creating a good painter.

Children with attention deficit disorder (ADD) usually exhibit considerable attention deficits in the logical-mathematical or linguistic areas but not always in the spatial or bodily-kinesthetic domains. This may not come as a surprise since the mathematical and linguistic disciplines require uninterrupted attention.

7. SUPPORT FROM PSYCHOMETRIC FINDINGS.

Validity of the multiple intelligence theory can be derived from results of the standardized measures such as the IQ tests. An individual may get a high score on IQ sub-tests dealing with words (vocabulary) but a low score on those relating to numbers (arithmetic) or pictures and images (object assembly or picture arrangement). These observations help prove the relative autonomy of logical-mathematical and linguistic intelligences.

Unfortunately, however, quantitative measures of intelligence exist for only two types: linguistic and logical-mathematical. Because the theory of multiple intelligence is rather new (1983) such measures do not yet exist for musical, body-kinesthetic, and personal intelligences.

8. SUSCEPTIBILITY TO ENCODING IN A SYMBOL SYSTEM.

Humans have the unique ability to express a thought about something "that is not immediately present to the senses." Armstrong, Ibid., 253. "The ability to symbolize … is the key faculty that separates human beings from … animals." Man can bring back to present something through the use of gesture, a sound, or a mark on a piece of paper. Symbols enabled us of entering into the thoughts of people who lived thousands of years ago. The monuments, wall paintings, and artifacts left by the Ancient Egyptians provide the proof of a "civilization of learning and skill." Safwat Bishara and Dawlat Bishara, ABOUT LEARNING AND EDUCATION. A PARENT AND EDUCATOR'S VEW SUPPORTED BY OVERSEAS EXPERIENCE, Authorhouse, Bloomington, IN, 2015, 159 – 179.

The following are the 'languages' in which humanity has chosen to symbolize its world.

a. Linguistic: Written and spoken languages.

b. Logical-mathematical: Number systems, computer languages.
c. Spatial: Ideographic languages (e. g., picture aspects of Chinese, hieroglyphics which also have phonetic components); line, shape, and color in art.
d. Bodily-kinethetic: Languages of dance, sports.
e. Musical: Musical notations.
f. Interpersonal: Gestures, facial expressions, body postures, and voice tones.
g. Intrapersonal: Dream symbols that reveal some aspects of the self.

The seven types (Gardner later added two: Naturalist and Existential) of intelligences identified under the theory of multiple intelligence share the above eight criteria to qualify as separate, autonomous entities. Each person has at least one dominant type in addition to varying levels of the other types. For example, a good mathematician might also love music, or an athlete might enjoy painting.

The next several chapters discuss each type of the seven intelligences.

CHAPTER 7

VERBAL INTELLIGENCE

Communication between human beings was the corner stone in building societies and civilizations. Languages allowed man to communicate his experiences across space and time. The written language has allowed humanity to record its history, knowledge, and discoveries. In essence, language ultimately represents one of man's most intelligent forms of behavior.

Language has different functions. It has the potential to excite, convince, stimulate, convey information, or just to please.

The invention of writing took place around the Fourth Millenium B.C. The Ancient Egyptians "used hieroglyphics to record the various aspects of their lives. They selected 24 hieroglyphs for 24 different consonant sounds and added others to represent clusters of consonants. They almost created an alphabet." Bishara and Bishara, ABOUT LEARNING AND EDUCATION, Ibid., 171.

Armstrong believes that linguistic intelligence is perhaps "the most universal of the seven intelligences in MI theory." 7 KINDS OF SMART. Ibid., 27. In the American culture language ability is the most highly regarded intelligence, right beside the logical-mathematical thinking. Both types of intelligence form the core of the IQ test.

Howard Gardner states that "linguistic competence is … the intelligence—the intellectual competence—that seems widely and most democratically shared across the human species." FRAMES OF MIND, Basic Books, New York, N.Y., 2011, 82.

Linguistic mastery is widely thought to involve special processes of acquisition that differ from those entailed in other types of intelligence. Noam Chomsky claims that children must be born with 'innate knowledge' about the rules of language. Chomsky's hypothesis is based on the fact that it is difficult to explain how language can be acquired so rapidly and so accurately at a time when children's other problem-solving skills are relatively still underdeveloped.

To be sure, linguistic intelligence is more complex than parroting back answers on a standardized test. A language has several components that include phonology, syntax, semantics, and pragmatics.

An individual with high linguistic intelligence has a sharp sensitivity to the sounds or phonology of the language. This is usually accompanied by a clever way of manipulating the structure or syntax of language. He also has a deep appreciation of its meaning or semantics. But probably the most crucial component of linguistic intelligence is the capacity to use language to achieve practical goals, that is, the pragmatics of language. Though the language itself may not be first-rate, the purpose to which language is used serves to enhance or change lives in some way.

From infancy we learn to internalize verbal sounds to form what Armstrong calls an 'inner speech' that becomes a primary tool of our thought. Some people refer to this precess as self-talk—the interior monologue that is continuously going on below the surface of consciousness. Writers occasionally refer to this stream of consciousness as if there were someone in the vicinity actually communicating with them. Some writers have a notebook that represents a kind of link between his/her mind and the outside world. It helps the writer to externalize what goes on inside the verbal mind.

"The ability to process linguistic messages rapidly … seems to depend upon an intact left temporal lobe … the abnormal development of his neural zone generally suffice to produce language impairments," writes Gardner, Ibid., 88. Albert Einstein is said to have begun to speak very late, but this might have allowed him to view the world in a less conventionalized way.

Unilateral injury to the brain have linguistic consequences that have been studied over the century. It is possible now to specify legions that cause particular difficulties in "phonological discrimination, in the pragmatic uses of speech, and, most critically, in the semantic and syntactic aspects of language … each of these aspects … can be destroyed in relative isolation." Gardner, Ibid., 91.

Oral and written forms of language share some core capacities. But specific additional skills are needed for someone to express himself appropriately in writing. As an individual becomes more skilled in one means of expression, it may become more difficult for him to excel in the other. (The author of this work is a poor speaker.)

Writing a book poses organizational skills that are different from those entailed in shorter linguistic pieces such as spoken performances, or a letter, or a poem.

Reading and writing go hand in hand. The first is a basis for excelling in the second. But we have a widespread problem about the lack of interest in reading. "More than 20 million adults cannot read menus, signs, or other simple printed matter. Another 40 million can function only at a fourth-grade reading level." Armstrong, Ibid., 35. The negative social and political implications of these statistics can not be overemphasized.

A Gallup poll says that each day Americans watch television an average of two and a half hours, listen to radio for almost two hours, and read for only about twenty minutes. Furthermore, the literature Americans read is often not of the highest quality. The National Endowment for the Arts says that only 7 to twelve percent of the population reads serious literature by novelists such as Dickens, Hemingway, and others. Our culture apparently places low value on personal reading.

Marc Peyser writes that "reading isn't just filling your head—it's nourishing it." READERS DIGEST, March 2019, 122 – 124. Reading is the perfect brain food, believes Peyser. Some people try to improve their memory and cognitive functions by taking fish oil supplements, eat lots of turmeric, invest in puzzle books, or spend a few hours exercising very week. But, the "cheapest, easiest, and most time-tested way to sharpen your brain … [is] reading." Ibid., 122.

Reading mostly impacts the area associated with language

reception, the left temporal cortex. "Processing written material—from the letters to the words to the sentences to the stories themselves—snaps the neurons to attention as they start work of transmitting all that information. That happens when we process spoken language, too, but the very nature of reading encourages the brain to work harder and better." Dr. Maryanne Wolf, director of the UCLA Center for Dyslexia, Diverse Learners, and Social Justice says "Typically, when you read, you have more time to think."

To put it differently, reading gives you a unique pause button for comprehension and insight.

Reading also energizes the region responsible for motor activity, the central sulcus. This may not be surprising since the brain is a "very exuberant play actor." Ibid., 123. When you are reading about a physical activity, the neurons responsible for controlling this activity get involved as well. The more parts of your brain that get a workout, the better it is for your overall cognitive performance.

Research conducted at Stanford University show that serious literary reading gives the brain a major workout. "MRI scans of people who are deep into a Jane Austen novel showed an increase in blood flowing to areas of the brain that control both cognitive and executive function, as opposed to the more limited effects that come from more leisurely reading." Ibid., 124.

Underestimating the benefits of reading is occurring at a time when the amount of available information has exploded. From the invention of writing six thousand years ago till the introduction of the first printing press in 1457, books were hand written. The number of books on a single topic was usually limited to one copy. The loss of such a copy was a serious blow to human knowledge. The Library of Alexandria, Egypt, was "one of the largest and most significant libraries of the ancient world." WICKIPEDIA ENCYCLOPEDIA. The library is famous for having "been burnt, around 270 A.D., together with most of the precious records of human history and achievement. The fire resulted in the loss of many scrolls and books, and has become a symbol of a destroyed culture. The link between the Ancient Egyptian civilization and the advancement of knowledge was cut off." Bishara and Bishara, ABOUT LEARNING AND EDUCATION, Authorhouse, Bloomington, IN, 2015, 169.

Five hundred years after the invention of printing, a second explosion of knowledge dawned on humanity through the Internet late in the twentieth century. Now, tremendous amount of information is right at the finger tips of everyone. Many rely on the Internet as *the* source of knowledge.

This has created two problems. First, not all information on the Internet is accurate—no peer-reviewing process to guarantee correctness of data. Anyone with access to a computer can put whatever information s/he thinks is worthy. Second, the availability of instantaneous access to data (though of doubtful reliability) renders it unnecessarily tedious to search real resources of dependable information.

It takes a lot of interest and determination for individuals today to get serious reading material put together by intellectuals and specialists in the field of interest.

CHAPTER 8

SPATIAL INTELLIGENCE

The architect can 'see' how a building would look like after it has been built. The engineer has the ability to visualize how the project would come through after the various components had been put together. A painter enjoys transforming a visual image from his/her mind onto the canvas.

Howard Gardner refers to this type of intelligence as spatial intelligence. The individual has "the power of focused perception to reveal what is present—though hidden to the casual observer—in all things visible." Armstrong, Ibid., 45. It also includes "the capacity to perform transformations on one's initial perceptions."

A spatially-intelligent person sees things—whether in the tangible world or in the mind—that others usually miss. The sculptor can make mental rotations and transformations of some subjective images.

In other words, the intricate perception of the visual world is the core feature of spatial intelligence. This usually combines with the ability to "perform transformations and modifications upon one's initial perceptions," Gardner, Ibid., 182.

The ability to produce forms is different from those required to manipulate those forms that have been provided. An individual may be acute in visual perception while having less ability to draw, imagine, or transform an absent object. That is, spatial intelligence comes in as an amalgam of abilities. Spatial intelligence can develop even in a person who is blind and therefore has no direct connection to the visual world. This indicates that spatial knowledge is not totally dependent upon the visual system; blind individuals can appreciate some aspects of pictures.

Spatial intelligence of adults have long been recognized. But little has been established about the development of this talent in children.

Only Jean Piaget did conduct several studies in this realm. He sensed a distinction between *figurative* knowledge and *operative* knowledge. That is, there is a difference between retaining the configuration of an object (a mental image) and the transformation of this configuration (manipulation of such an image). Put differently, Piaget separated the static configuration from the active operation

"Children may know their way around many areas in their neighborhood …. Yet they often will lack the capacity to provide a map … or an overall verbal account of the relationship among several spots …. While children's spatial understanding develops space, the expression of this understanding via another intelligence or symbolic code remains difficult." Gardner, Ibid., 190.

This illustrates God's wisdom manifest in His creation. The child has enough visual-spatial intelligence to help him/her to find the way in the surroundings or in the neighborhood. But he can not connect these spots, or express the visual imagery into another coded system. This limited capacity helps keep the youngster close to the parents where he finds protection and support. As he grows up to be stronger and more independent, the ability to act on, or manipulate, the visual imagery has developed into the capacity to express his understanding of space into another coded system like drawing a map or providing a verbal account of the relationship between several spots.

Whereas spatial intelligence in children has been neglected, it has received the most widespread attention second only to linguistic intelligence

The left hemisphere of the brain is the site of linguistic processing, while the right hemisphere proves to be the site most crucial for spatial (and visual-spatial) processing. However, the right hemisphere is not "quite so decisive in the case of spatial processing as the left hemisphere is for language." Gardner, Ibid., 190. Sizable shortages in spatial ability can also follow upon damage to the left side of the brain.

Some of the people with spatial intelligence have a hawk-eyed ability that makes them able to see at distances far beyond the optical standard of 20/20 vision. Veronica Seider, a German student, could identify persons at a distance of more than a mile.

Alternatively, some spatially intelligent people posses remarkable observation skills for objects at closer range. Eskimo hunters give extreme attention to small details in the shape of ice and snow under their feet. This is a matter of life or death. Any mistake can take them onto a floating sheet of ice that might break off and leave them stranded in the middle of nowhere.

Individuals gifted with spatial intelligence may have a keen observation for beauty. This is specially evident in the spatial intelligence of the interior decorator, the landscape architect, the sculptor, the artist, or the art critic. They have high sensitivity to certain features of a artistic work such as line, shape, space, volume, color, balance, light and shade, harmony, and pattern.

Art can have a tremendous power on the human psyche. Some, though not many, individuals are sensitive enough to the point that classic masterpieces of painting or sculptor in a museum can cause "rapid heart beat, emotional upheaval, fainting, and even hallucinations." Armstrong, Ibid., 49.

Spatial intelligence is not just looking outwardly at the visible world. It also includes the turning inward and transforming of such perceptions. The eye sees first, then interacts with the mind to create subjective visual images. Though the process is still little understood by scientists, it represents a significant way for some individuals to create, remember, and process information. The images they formed may near the quality of photographic prints.

People with such talent can look at a picture, form an internal image, then with eyes still closed, scan that image for additional details not observed in the original viewing of the picture.

The neurophysiologist W. Gray Walter says that about one-sixth of a normal population sees vivid inner imagery, another sixth does not use visual images in their thinking process unless thy are required to do so, and the remaining two thirds can evoke satisfactory visual patterns when necessary.

Intelligent visualization helps "the stimulation of creative potentials and the cultivation of higher-order thinking processes." Armstrong, Ibid., 55. Rudolf Arnheim of Harvard University claims that practically *all* thinking— even the most theoretical and abstract—is visual in nature.

Routine tests of spatial thinking in normal adults show that they often exhibit a decrease in their performance. But, at the same time, individuals with high spatial abilities perform very well until the end of their lives.

Gardner believes that each type of intelligence has a natural life course. Logical-mathematical abilities becomes fragile later in life across all people. Same is true of the bodily-kinesthetic intelligence which shows signs of risk with age. On the other hand, certain aspects of visual and spatial thinking "prove robust, especially in individuals who have practiced them regularly throughout their lives." Ibid., 215. The sense of the whole—central in spatial intelligence—endures time and seems to be a reward for aging. They show an enhanced capacity to "appreciate the whole, to discern patterns even when certain details or fine points may be lost. Perhaps wisdom draws on this sensitivity to patterns, forms, and whole."

CHAPTER 9

BODILY-KINESTHETIC INTELLIGENCE

Bodily intelligence encompasses two aspects. The first is the ability to use one's own body in "highly differentiated and skilled ways, for expressive as well as goal-directed purposes." Gardner, Ibid., 218. We see this when a person runs, climb, or prop up a heavy load. The second is the capacity to work skillfully with objects. This skill is manifested when an individual involves "the motor movements of one's fingers and hands and those that exploit gross motor movements of the body."

The capacities to control one's bodily motions and to handle objects skillfully are the cores of bodily intelligence. It is possible for these two core components to exist separately in one and the same individual.

However, people in whom use of the body is central— such as actors—other intelligences ordinarily play a significant role. For the actor or the performer, skills in personal intelligences enhances the bodily intelligence. The same applies in the case of musical or linguistic presentations where personal intelligences are a welcome addition.

Our recent culture tended to make a distinction between physical activities exerted by our bodies and those activities associated with reasoning. That is, we divorced the *physical* from the *mental* based on a notion that what we do with our bodies is somehow less special than those problem-solving skills carried out mainly through the use of logic, language, or other symbolic systems.

But think of the pianist. A talented pianist can produce independent patterns of movement in each hand, "sustain different rhythms in each hand, while also using the two hands together to 'speak to one another' or to produce a fugal effect." Gardner, Ibid., 221.

A veteran soccer trainer in Wichita, Kansas, emphasized to his team that 90 percent of this sport is mental. Moving the ball is trivial compared with the mental requirement.

A crucial question related to bodily intelligence is the brain's role in physical activity. Roger Sperry, the renowned American neuropsychologist, points out that mental activity should be looked upon as a means to the end of executing actions. Gardner quotes Sperry who believes that thinking should be looked upon as a means of bringing "into motor behavior additional refinement, increased direction toward distant, future goals and greater overall adaptivity and survival value."

It is not only the mind, and the nervous system, that participate in one way or the other in the execution of motor actions but in fact most segments of the body do contribute to such activities. Muscles, joints, and tendons are directly involved; our kinesthetic sense allows us to judge the timing, force, and extent of our movements.

The opposite is also true. Armstrong points out that physical movement seems to be a significant factor in enhancing thinking processes. Ibid., 85. Some creative thinkers have reported that walking or running boosted their cognitive abilities.

As a support for posing bodily intelligence as a separate form of intelligence is the fact that injuries to zones of the left hemisphere known to be dominant for motor activity can produce selective impairment in bodily movements. A person can be physically able to carry out a set of motor sequences, and cognitively able to understand a request to do them, is nonetheless unable to carry them out in the proper order or in a proper manner.

Interestingly, such lapses—an inappropriate execution or an omitted action—are also found in normal persons, especially when they are functioning under pressure.

At the extreme, there are patients who are normal but can carry out virtually no actions at all. They exhibit an absence of bodily intelligence in its essentially pure form.

Here, too, the opposite is true. There are neuropsychological patients whose logical and linguistic abilities have been devastated but who show no difficulty in carrying out highly skilled motor movements.

Bodily intelligence is thought to develop since infancy. Although Jean Piaget did not relate his work to bodily intelligence, his description of the unfolding of sensori-motor intelligence illuminates its initial stages. Piaget described how infants progress from the simple reflexes, such as those involved in sucking and looking, to some behavioral movements that increasingly aim to fulfill individual intentions. That is, separate acts are combined to satisfy new goals. With time, the child starts to operate upon mental representations such as symbols. Now the use of tools has been coupled with the realm of pure thought.

Gardner, Ibid., 233, cites the work of Jerome Bruner and Kurt Fischer who support the idea that the development of skills "ought to be conceived of generally, not merely with reference to the bodily activities but rather with respect to all manners of cognitive operations. … [They] construe the development of knowledge as a building up of more elaborate and increasingly flexible skills … [that] become the … constituent acts of ever higher and more complex skills."

To illustrate, consider how the child first combines sucking and looking into grasping; the grasping of a single object develops into the passing of objects from one hand to the other. The child then learns how to use sets of objects to build simple structures that become more elaborate displays as s/he gets older.

Researchers such as Frederic Bartlett see no sharp distinction between physical acts and thinking skills. Physical actions are connected to some mental processes. They look upon the development of skills such as chess playing or computer programming as a manifestation of increasing mastery of various types and levels of skill.

However, it has been reported that some neurological disorders may bring a dissociation between symbolic capacities and motor activities. This suggests that physical activities may operate, to some degree, independent of the symbolic functions.

The complexity of the human body can not be overestimated. Among the different organs, the mind comes at the top in its complexity both structurally as well as functionally.

Bodily intelligence, according to Gardner, is a part of a trio of object-related intelligences: i- logical-mathematical intelligence which is the patterning of objects into numerical forms; ii- spatial intelligence which deals with the person's ability to transform objects within his/her environment and to figure out his way through a world of objects in space; and iii- bodily intelligence which includes both the movement of one's own body as well as physical actions on the objects in the world.

But the human body is more than simply a machine— even one with a *mind.* The body is "the vessel of the individual's sense of self, his most personal feelings and aspirations." Gardner, Ibid., 249.

CHAPTER 10

MUSICAL INTELLIGENCE

Of all the talents endowed by the Creator on man, music intelligence emerges the earliest in a person's life.

The core gift of music competence may well be inherited, but the extent to which the talent is manifested will depend upon the milieu in which one lives.

"When Wolfgang Amadeus Mozart was a baby, he visited the Sistine Chapel in Rome and was entranced by piece of music he heard there." Armstrong, Ibid., 67. The Vatican decreed that this musical work could be performed only inside the Chapel and could not never be copied. Mozart's response was to attend once more the performance of the piece. He then returned to his home and copied the entire work from memory.

Mozart later said when he composed music he could hear all of the notes of his composition simultaneously.

Composers present the 'end state' of musical intelligence. They make their adult livelihood using the skills lavishly bestowed on them.

"Working with tones, rhythms, and, above all, an overall sense of form and movement, the composer must decide how much sheer repetition, and which harmonic, melodic, rhythmic, or contrapuntal variations, are necessary to realize his conception." Gardner, Ibid., 108.

Aaron Copland, the composer, explains that composing is as natural as eating or sleeping. Wagner said he composed like a cow producing milk, and Saint-Saens likened the process of composing to an apple tree producing apples. Arnold Schoenberg states that "Whatever happens in a piece of music is nothing but the endless reshaping of a basic Shape."

To the naturally gifted, composing seems to be effortless. It just comes naturally. Composers agree on the naturalness of the act of composition. They, too, have considerable agreement about the fact that language plays no role in the act of composition. Roger Sessions explains that "at no time in the course of the actual process of composition were words involved …. In no way, however, did these words [told to the friend] help me—nor they have helped me— to find the precise pattern that I was seeking." Gardner, Ibid., 109.

Igor Stravinsky says that composing is doing, not thinking. Composing occurs not by acts of thought but is accomplished naturally. Arnold Schoenberg stresses the point that it is the musical material that must be dealt with. He states "I do not believe a composer can compose if you give him numbers instead of tones." It has been said that composers have minds that 'secrete music.'

Andre Previn, who died on February 28, 1989, was a composer, conductor, pianist, and musical director. He won 10 Grammy Awards and was knighted by Queen Elizabeth

II in 1996. His work ranged from classical and Jazz to the popular fare of Broadway and Hollywood. A prodigy child, Previn began working on MGM film scores while still in high school. In 1967 he was named musical director of the Houston Symphony, then later lead the London and Pillsburg symphonies. TIME, March 18, 2019, p. 13.

Conductors interpret the work of composers, whereas instrumentalists or singers perform composers' written work. Aaron Copland believes that the skills involved in listening to music have an unmistakable link to those involved in musical creation.

Musically inclined individuals fall within a wide range. There may be a hierarchy of difficulty involved as one moves from one end of the spectrum to the other: Performing requiring more demands than listening does, and composing exacting much more (or at least different) demands than performing.

Understanding the biological underpinnings of musical intelligence has been enhanced by studying bird singing. Gardner points to bird song as a skill located in the left part of the avian nervous system. "A lesion there will destroy bird song, whereas comparable lesions in the right half of the brain exert much less debilitating effects." Ibid., 123.

Obviously, the purposes of bird singing are different from those of human singing. (The Psalmist says that birds glorify God by their singing.) Yet the mechanism underlying the arrangement of certain core musical components in birds may well prove similar to those enjoyed by human beings.

There has always been the nagging question of whether

there are analogies between human music and language? At some point, however, researchers working with both normal and brain-damaged persons have proved, beyond a reasonable doubt, that the mechanisms controlling human music and language are distinctive from one another. Each talent is autonomous.

Diana Deutsch has shown that the mechanisms by which "pitch is apprehended and stored are different from the mechanisms that process other sounds, particularly those of language." Ibid., 124. Individuals were given a set of tones to remember and then presented with different interfering material. If the interfering material was other tones, recall for the initial set is seriously interfered with (in one study error was 40 percent). However, if the interfering material is verbal—for example, numbers—subjects could deal with even larger amounts of interference without much detectable effect on the memory for pitch (two percent error in the same study).

Like for other types of intelligence, the study of individuals whose brains have been damaged due to a stroke or other kinds of trauma provides dramatic confirmation of the uniqueness of musical perception. Research has found that a person can suffer serious verbal disability without any discernible musical impairment. Similarly, one can become disabled musically but still retaining his/her fundamental linguistic competences.

Gardner notes that linguistic abilities are almost exclusively located in the left hemisphere in right-handed individuals, whereas the majority of musical capacities are lateralized in the right hemisphere of most normal people.

Therefore, injury to the right hemisphere causes serious difficulties in discriminating tones, while injuries to the left hemisphere generally leave musical capacities relatively unaffected. Disease of the right hemisphere seems to compromise the appreciation of music.

When it comes to human beings generalizations are hard to come by. Cases have been reported that prove the existence of a great variety of musical syndromes even within the same population.

Some composers (Maurice Ravel) have suffered a musical disorder following the onset of aphasia (inability to express and understand written and spoken language). On the other hand, the Russian composer Shebalin continued to compose perfectly despite a severe case of aphasia. Certain musicians exhibited difficulties in the ability to perceive and criticize musical performances following injury to the *left* hemisphere.

Musical talent and capacity varies considerably in mankind. The variation is attributed to at least two factors. First, the tremendous range of types and degrees of musical skill. Second, individuals' initial encounter with music occurs through different media and modalities, and they continue to encounter music in peculiar and individual forms: singing, playing instruments by hand, inserting instruments into the mouth, reading of musical notation, listening to records, watching dances, or the like. Whereas exposure to music may take different avenues, exposure to natural language occurs primarily through listening to others speak.

The autonomy of musical competence becomes

evident as one considers the unique patterns of its breakdown. If destroyed, other abilities remain intact. The early appearance of musical intelligence in otherwise unremarkable individuals is another proof of its autonomy. The literature reports on quite a few cases of astonishing musical and acoustical achievements carried out by autistic youngsters. There are also cases where an otherwise normal child displays an exceptional ability in the musical realm.

Interestingly, "even the most gifted young child will take about ten years to achieve those levels of performance or composition that we associate with mastery of the musical realm," notes Gardner, Ibid., 128.

Like linguistic intelligence, musical competence is autonomous. The two types of intelligence are different from one another. Yet, they both share some common aspects. Each can proceed without relation to physical objects in the world. Both can be elaborated to a considerable degree simply through exploration and exploitation of the oral-auditory system. However, the musical talent develops neurologically in distinct ways from those of the linguistic intelligence.

Many composers felt strongly that music has close ties to bodily language. Some tend to think of music as an extended gesture—a movement that is carried out, at least implicitly, with the body. Young children find it virtually impossible to sing without engaging some physical activity.

A study by Chia-Jung Tsay, a concert pianist who is also a researcher at University College, London, found that "even judges awarding prizes can be swayed by what they see as well as what they hear." TOP MUSICIANS ARE

JUDGES AS MUCH FOR THEIR MOVEMENTS AS FOR THEIR MELODIES. THE ECONOMIST, August 24, 2013, 71, 72. The study, published in the NATIONAL ACADEMY OF SCIENCES, found that even the experts could not screen out "historic flummery on the part of performers." The article advises musicians to brush up on their stage skills as well as their musical ones.

We celebrate our most significant rites of passage—weddings and funerals—with music. We "exercise to music, worship to music, and shop to music," writes Armstrong, Ibid., 63.

Music seems to be also tied up to spatial intelligence, even though the relationship may not be immediately evident. Both spatial and musical intelligences are localized in the right hemisphere. Psychologist Lauren Harris reported on claims that "composers are dependent upon powerful spatial abilities, which are required to posit, appreciate, and revise the complex architectonic of a composition." Gardner, Ibid., 130. The contemporary Greek composer Yanni is a vivid example.

The connection between musical performance and the feelings of persons is universally acknowledged. And feelings have a pivotal role in the personal intelligences. Music is a logical avenue for capturing feelings, knowledge about feelings, or knowledge about the forms of feeling, communicating them from the performer or the composer to the careful listener.

Amazingly, a person who had suffered extensive right hemisphere damage retained his abilities to teach music and even write books about it but refrained from composing because he realized that he could no longer recall the feeling of the whole piece, nor the sense of what worked and what did not work.

Whereas Howard Gardner is convinced of the autonomy of each of the music and the language competences, musicologists and well-informed musicians like Leonard Bernstein continue to search for non-negligible parallels between music and language. But these opponents are also quick to say that not all aspects of language are directly analogous to music. For example, the semantic aspect of language is largely underdeveloped in music; and the notion of strict grammatical rules is irrelevant in music, where violations of these rules are often prized.

Since medieval times, many careful students of music noted that music shared many features with the principles of mathematics, such as proportions, special ratios, recurring patterns, and other detectable series. With time, as harmonic concerns gained in ascendancy, the mathematical aspects of music became less obvious. In the twentieth century, the relationship between musical and mathematical abilities has been largely pondered.

To appreciate rhythms in musical work, the person must have some basic numerical thinking. The sensitivity to regularity and ratios in performances can sometimes be complex. This basic competence, however, turns into a somewhat higher mathematical thought when it comes to "an appreciation of basic musical structures, and of how they can be repeated, transformed, embedded, or otherwise played off one against another." Gardner, Ibid., 133.

Musicians like Bach, Schumann, and Mozart showed great sensitivity to mathematical patterns and regularities.

The pure mathematician is concerned with forms for their own sake, in their own implications, apart from any particular communicative purpose. The musician, on the other hand, deals with patterned elements which must appear in sounds that are firmly put together in certain ways not to fulfill formal considerations but because they have expressive power and effect on the listener.

The mathematician G. H. Hardy noted that it was music that could stimulate emotions, accelerate the pulse, cure the course of asthma, induce epilepsy, or calm an infant.

It may not be surprising to find superficial links between aspects of music and properties of other intellectual systems. The probability of finding some analogies between any two intelligences is high.

Gardner strongly believes that the core operations of music do not have strong connections to the core operations in other types of intelligences, and therefore musical talent deserves to be considered as an autonomous intellectual system.

C H A P T E R 11

LOGICAL MATHEMATICAL INTELLIGENCE

Unlike the musical and linguistic talents, logical-mathematical intelligence does not originate in the auditory-oral sphere. It starts as an interaction with the world of objects.

Gardner summarizes the course of development of mathematical-logical thinking from "objects to statements, from actions to the relations among actions, from the realm of the sensori-motor to the realm of pure abstraction—ultimately to the heights of logic and science." Ibid., 136.

An explanation is here due. The preeminent research of the Swiss developmental psychologist Jean Piaget provides the path-breaking understanding of this type of intelligence. Piaget has been extensively devoted to the study of children.

In the first months of a child's life s/he explores different objects: nipples, rattles, and cups. These objects are tied up to his moment-to-moment experience with them, and so when they disappear from his sight, he no longer has conscious memory of them.

After the child grows to be about eighteen months, he becomes aware of the fact that objects will continue to exist even if they have been removed from his time-and-space world. The sense that objects have existence regardless of one's particular action upon them is termed 'object permanence.' This realization is a cornerstone for later mental development.

The child also becomes able to notice the similarities among certain objects—for example, all trucks, all red cars, are grouped together because they possess same identifiable properties. This signals the recognition of a *class* or *set.*

But the child still lacks the knowledge that there exists a regular number system, with each number representing one more than the previous one; and that any set of objects has a definite quantity.

The quantitative sense comes into play at the age of four or five. Even though the child may be able to count and recite the number series before reaching that age, this ability is essentially a manifestation of linguistic intelligence. But, with the onset of the quantitative ability, the child learns that the number series can be applied to arrays of objects.

At the age of six or seven the child reaches the level of young mathematician-to-be as Piaget calls it. Given two sets of objects and asked which pile has the greater number, s/he will not be misled by the wider space over which a pile might be spread. He will count the number of objects in each pile and reach the correct conclusion. He has arrived at a relatively foolproof method of assessing quantity.

This critical stage denotes the child's ability to contrast the number in one set to the number in another, even if the sets are different in appearance, and even if both are not available for inspection. The child has in fact reached a level of being able to create two mental images.

The child can now make additional operations. He can *add* the same number of constituents to each pile, and the result of the two additions will yield identical sums. The same would happen if he *subtract* equal amounts from each set. Multiplying and dividing come later.

So, the initial stages of logical-mathematical intelligence that involves manipulation of physical objects evolves into mental operations that become increasingly certain.

At the age of seven to ten, logical necessity becomes an integral part of these processes. Certain rules of logic exist and must apply. Two piles *must* remain the same because you haven't added or taken anything away, and not just because they have equal number of objects.

During the early years of adolescence the normal child becomes capable of formal mental operations. Now he can deal with objects, mental images or models of these objects, words, symbols, or strings of symbols (equations) that represent objects, and actions on objects. "Where once his physical actions transformed objects, now mental operations transform sets of symbols." Gardener, Ibid., 139. "These symbol-manipulating capacities prove 'of the essence' in higher branches of mathematics, with the symbols standing for objects, relations, functions, or other operations." The symbols to be manipulated may also be words, as in the case of logical reasoning, and scientific hypothesis formation.

Recent studies, however, show that "only 30 to 40

percent of the adolescent and adult population in our culture use formal operational thinking. And it is often not used even by those who have the capacity to think in this way." Armstrong, Ibid., 98.

Logical reasoning is not the same as the rhetorical language encountered in linguistic intelligence. Whereas one can make logical inferences that are consistent with common sense, the rules of reasoning can be equally applied to apparently unrelated statements. To put it differently, correct inferences can only be drawn when the statements are treated like elements (or objects) to be manipulated not as meaningful phrases to be thought of. Such *higher level* operations become possible only during adolescence. However, not all individuals continue to be able to follow all the processes of reasoning in the chain.

Gardner points out clearly that the foregoing analysis of Jean Piaget is the best "worked-out trajectory of growth in all of developmental psychology." Ibid., 140. But Gardner does not agree with Piaget's theory that "logical-mathematical thought is the glue that holds together all cognition." Although Piaget has suggested a brilliant view of development in the logical-mathematical thinking, he mistakenly assumed that it carries over to other areas ranging from musical intelligence to the interpersonal domain.

Howard Gardner cites recent research that has well documented the notion that development in the logical-mathematical arena is "less regular, lock-step, and stage like" than Piaget thought. Steps are more gradual and heterogeneous. It seems that when it comes to human beings, generalizations usually carry some risk. Individuality of man is an integral part of God's creation.

It is also evident that Piaget's picture of higher operational thought applies mainly to the mainstream of Western middle-class persons.

But the points of contention with Piaget's hypotheses should not distract from his accomplishment in discerning the origins of logical-mathematical intelligence

> "the child's actions upon the physical world; the crucial importance of the discovery of numbers; the gradual transition from physical manipulation of objects to interiorized transformations of actions; the significance of relations among actions themselves; and the special nature of higher tiers of development, where the individual begins to work with hypothetical statements and to explore the relationships and implications that obtain among those statements." Gardner, Ibid., 141.

Needless to say, the realms of numbers, mathematics, logic, and science are not the same. It is true that they form a family of interrelated abilities, and Piaget's enduring achievements is to have proposed some of the integrated links between them.

It has rightfully been said that mathematics is the only discipline that stands by itself. Physics depends on mathematics; chemistry depends on physics and mathematics; biology depends on chemistry, physics, and mathematics; geology depends on biology, chemistry, physics, and mathematics. The late, well-known mathematician G. H. Hardy said that "a mathematician has no materials to work with, and so his patterns are likely to last longer, since ideas erase less well than works do." Gardner, Ibid., 147.

Mathematicians were able to predict the existence of new elements in the Periodic Table of Elements. Their calculations proved true years later when chemists established the experimental proof that these elements do actually exist.

The relationships between mathematics and the various disciplines of science is rather simple when compared with that between mathematics and logic.

Willard Quine, the renowned logician of the first half of the twentieth century, explained that logic is about statements while mathematics deals with abstract, non linguistic entities, but that logic at its higher reaches leads by natural stages into mathematics. In fact, mathematics at its highest levels rarely use numbers. Mathematicians are basically looking for general concepts by formulating rules that can apply to the widest possible range of problems.

Alfred N. Whitehead and Russell Bertrand sought to show that "underlying even the most complex mathematical statements, one can find simple logical properties—the sort of intuition that the child is beginning to display as his operational thinking unfolds." Gardner, Ibid., 142. Russell noted that logic and mathematics are one; they differ as boy and man where logic is the youth of mathematics and mathematics is the manhood of logic.

Mathematicians, at higher levels, work with invented objects and symbols to reach concepts that usually have no direct parallel in everyday life, just as the logicians who are primarily interested in relationships among statements rather than the relation of those statements to the world of reality. On the other hand, the scientist, by definition, retains the direct relationship to the world of practice. He comes up with "statements, models, and theories which, in addition to being logically consistent and susceptible to mathematical treatment, must also bear a justifiable and continuing relationship to facts which have been (and will be) discovered about the world." Gardner, Ibid., 143.

But not everyone agrees with Russell's view that logic and mathematics are one. Henri Poincare', the leading mathematician in the world at the turn of the twentieth century, raised the question: If mathematics only involves the rules of logic, which are likely to be acceptable by all normal minds, then why should anyone have difficulty in understanding mathematics?

Poincare' explains

> "A mathematical demonstration is not simply a single juxtaposition of syllogisms, it is syllogisms placed in a certain order, and the order in which these elements are placed is much more important than the elements themselves." Gardner, Ibid., 145.

Poincare' then reaches the conclusion that there are two distinct abilities. One is sheer memory for steps in a chain of reasoning. The other, and more important, ability is an appreciation and understanding of the nature of the links between the propositions where the conclusion of each one serves as the premise for the next.

Alfred Adler, the renowned mathematician, notes that in mathematics, those with true talent are discovered almost immediately. The characteristics of the mathematically blessed are so evident that they leave little room for jealously, bitterness, or reservations as may be the normal case in other disciplines.

While the mental powers central to any discipline are spread out unequally between the population, there are few fields other than mathematics where the extremes are so great.

The mathematician loves to deal with abstraction. He must be rigorous and perennially skeptical; no fact is readily accepted unless proved by steps that are derived from universally accepted principles. Although the mathematician has great freedom in creating any kind of system he wants, in the end any mathematical theory must agree with physical reality. As mentioned earlier, physics is essentially dependent upon mathematics, and a mathematical theory should not contradict the laws of physics.

Quite possibly, "the most central and least replaceable feature of the mathematician's gift is the ability to handle skillfully long chains of reasoning …. Initially, this prosecution of an extended line of reasoning may be intuitive. Many mathematicians report that they sense a solution, or a direction, long before they have worked out each step in detail." Gardner, Ibid., 147.

For at least a century, the field of mathematics has become increasingly abstract. Alfred Adler provides details about how mathematics has developed from the simple to the complex.

The first abstraction is the idea of *numbers,* and the finding that different quantities can be distinguished from one another based on the number of each. Then comes the creation of *algebra,* where variables are introduced together with system of numbers. For example, when a + b = c, each variable can attain any number so long as the relationship remains valid. In mathematical *functions* the variables are no longer specialized cases but one variable has a systematic relation to another variable. For example, f (c) depends on a and b.

To put it differently, Adler notes that by generalizing the concept of numbers, then the concept of the variable, and finally that of the function, it is possible to arrive at an extremely abstract and general level of thinking. However, not every one feels comfortable dealing with the higher levels of abstraction and therefore there is a powerful pull toward finding simpler expressions and for returning to the fundamental principles of numbers.

Interestingly, one of the authors of this work happens to be a major in both mathematics and physics. She studied at the College of Science, Cairo University, Cairo. The curriculum involved studying four disciplines in the Freshman year: Pure Mathematics, Applied Mathematics, Physics, and Chemistry (no Humanities or Social Studies, or electives). In the Sophomore year, the student drops one of the four disciplines, and the total credit hours are divided between the other three: Pure Mathematics, Applied Mathematics, and Physics. In the Junior and Senior years, one more discipline is dropped and all credit hours are allotted to the two fields of Pure Mathematics and Physics.

She graduated near the top of her class with a "B" in Pure Mathematics and a "B" in Physics (it is extremely rare to get an "A" in any of these two subjects).

Over the 50-plus years of our marriage, it became obvious that Dawlat, the mathematician and physicist who went on to get an M. S. then a Ph. D. in Physics, does not feel comfortable dealing with, say, adding or subtracting simple numbers. Yet, she has always enjoyed abstraction at the highest levels of mathematics.

To major in Mathematics from Cairo University, the student study the following courses (credit hours are semester credit hours).

Freshman Year: Differential and Integral Calculus; three credit hrs.
Interpolation; one credit hr.
Higher Algebra and Analytical Geometry; three credit hrs.
Numerical Solution of Equations; four credit hrs.

Sophomore Year: Matrix Theory – Solid Geometry; three credit hrs.
Root Square Method and Numerical Integration; three credit hrs.
Differential and Integral Calculus – Infinite Series; three credit hrs.

Junior Year: Topology – Abstract Algebra; four credit hrs.
Projective Geometry; four credit hrs.
Differential Equations; five credit hrs.

Senior Year: Theory of Complex Variables; three credit hrs.
Abstract Algebra; three credit hrs.
Special Functions and Integral Functions; three credit hrs.
Differential Geometry; three credit hrs.

This adds up to 45 semester credit hours of Pure Mathematics in addition to 20 semester credit hours studying Applied Mathematics in the Freshman and Sophomore years. These courses cover Statics and Dynamics.

Here is an individual who went through, and did well, dealing with abstraction at the highest mathematical levels, yet does not enjoy dealing with numbers in its simplest forms of adding or subtracting. How marvelous is the human mind formed by the Creator of the universe!

From among the various disciplines, mathematics still has no Nobel prize. This is probably due to the fact that mathematical skills among those qualified differ in its essence: some are "much more given to the use and valuing of intuition, while others extol only systematic proof." Gardner, Ibid., 149.

Mathematicians, as well as scientists, share the interest of problem solving. They pose a problem then seek to solve it in the most efficient and effective way.

Since the seventeenth century, the marked progress of science can be attributed significantly to the invention of differential and integral calculus. Chemistry and Physics are concerned with the study and explanation of change.

Without calculus, one has to calculate every tiny step of the process. Applying differentiation and integration renders it possible to determine how the change of one variable relates to the other variables connected to it.

Mathematics with its abstract relations allows the scientist to make some order of the unwieldy body of brute fact. But there is a clear distinction between mathematics and the core fields of science such as physics and chemistry.

The mathematician is interested in exploring abstract systems for their own sake. The scientist seeks to explain physical reality. For him, mathematics is an indispensable tool for building models and theories that can describe and explain the operation of the world: physics and chemistry are concerned with material objects in this world; biology deals with the living objects; and cognitive science studies the human mind.

To put it differently, the world of mathematics is *ideal* whereas that of the scientist is *real.* For the mathematician the goal is to recognize patterns wherever they may exist; one follows his train of thinking wherever they may lead. The scientist's perpetual concern is the application of his ideas for the physical universe. Albert Einstein, who pursued both careers, explained: "Truth in physical matters can of course never be founded on mathematical and logical considerations alone." Gardner, Ibid., 155.

The greatest progress in science is achieved when disparate elements are linked together to yield a few simple rules that explain the observed interactions.

Werner Heisenberg, the Nobel laureate in physics at the age of thirty-two tells about his mentor Niels Bohr

"Bohr knows precisely how atoms behave during light emission, in chemical processes and in many other phenomena, and this has helped him to form an intuitive picture of the structure of different atoms." Gardner, Ibid., 156.

It has later been proved using the quantum theory that when an electron inside an atom moves from one energy level to another level, with lower energy, the difference is emitted as light. The atoms of each element emit light at a wavelength specific of that given element. Sodium atoms emit light at a wavelength different from those of, say, potassium.

Einstein spent years studying the absoluteness of time and space. He questioned what would happen if a person rides a beam of light as opposed to another individual looking at a clock. Because of the immense difference in the speed of travel, the time of that clock would remain frozen, or perpetually the same, while the other travels at the speed of light. That is, the experience of time would become different for the traveler on the light beam from what it was for the person remaining at home. He eventually arrived at the well-known equation: Energy (E) equals mass (m) multiplied by the square of the velocity of light (c). Because the velocity of light in vacuum is 2.99 multiplied by 10 to the power 8 meter/second, it is easy to calculate the amount of energy released even when a small amount of material is destroyed. The simple equation Einstein arrived at did unify the diverse phenomena of mass, speed of light, and energy.

About Isaac Newton, Frank Manuel wrote

"At the height of his powers there was in him a compelling desire to find order and deign in what appeared to be chaos, to distill from a vast inchoate mass of materials a few basic principles that would embrace the whole and define the relationships of its component parts.... he was searching for a unifying structure." Gardner, Ibid., 159.

Newton discovered that 'every object will remain at rest or in uniform motion in a straight line unless compelled to change its state by the action of an external force.' He also found that 'for every action (force) in nature there is an equal and opposite reaction.'

It was later discovered that Newton's laws apply to objects that have mass. The motion of subatomic particles, however, could be explained by the quantum theory. Electrons in an atom occupy certain, defined energy levels and when the atom is excited by an external force, an electron 'jumps' from its energy level to another orbit with a higher energy level. The opposite occurs when the source of excitation is removed. The point is that in response to external forces, the movement of electrons (objects with negligible mass that is considered to be zero for all practical calculations) within the atom is abrupt and not gradual.

Physical scientists share a passion for the single unifying relationship(s) that may offer overall explanations of the essence of life.

Just as mathematics is not simply simple arithmetic, science is not just a collection of boring facts—it is a set of patterns and basic laws that apply to many disciplines. James Trefil and Robert Hazen write "Science is organized around certain central concepts, certain pillars that support the entire structure. There are a limited number of such concepts ... but they account for everything we see in the world around us."

These laws are discovered and articulated by "the regularity-seeking, hypothesis-testing methodology of logical-mathematical intelligence." Armstrong, Ibid., 106.

The discovery of the Periodic Table of the Elements, around the turn of the twentieth century, has been a cornerstone in the field of chemistry. The 105 elements known to scientists as of the 1980s could be arranged in rows and columns that tabulate elements with similar properties in the same column. Instead of dealing with 105 different elements, each with different properties, the whole set was divided into eight groups; each group lists elements with similar properties that change regularly from one row to the next.

A distinct feature of mathematics is that the talent announces itself very early. The individual becomes immersed in patterns per se. The young child builds some satisfying experiences with numbers; then he experiments further with symbolic domains; and eventually the individual proceeds beyond his natural mathematical curiosity to get acquainted with problems that have challenged the mathematicians before him.

It has been noticed that in the field of mathematics, more so than in any other intellectual area, the thirties and forties are the optimum years of achievement. The ability to memorize and manipulate all the variables necessary to work on important mathematical problems is especially vulnerable to age. The information retrieval part of the mind apparently goes, along with the interconnections between the neurons.

Interestingly, a mathematician's ability to calculate rapidly is not a qualifying necessity. It may be an accidental advantage but nothing more. As mentioned earlier, the co-author of this work had a B. S. with a major in mathematics and physics that include 65 semester credit hours in Pure Mathematics and Applied Mathematics yet she does not think of herself as good in arithmetic. She did very well in courses such as Differential Equations, Theory of Complex Variables, Special Functions, and Differential Geometry—highest levels of abstraction.

Alternatively, idiot savants with meager or retarded abilities in most areas may be able to calculate very rapidly and very accurately. They do not use mathematics to help them in other areas of daily life, nor are they interested in discovering and solving new problems. Gardner tends to attribute the early arithmetical prodigiousness to the relative sparing of certain brain areas.

It is amazing how humans differ in their abilities. Some with otherwise normal abilities show selective weakness in the numerical realm. The numerical difficulty is akin to the difficulties exhibited by many children with written language (dyslexics) and by a smaller number with spoken language (dysphasics).

More is now known about the evolution of language and music than the antecedent numerical ability. And even less is known about its organization in the brain of normal human beings. Gardner hypothesized that "The ability to read and produce the signs of mathematics is more often a left hemisphere function whereas the understanding of numerical relations and concepts seems to entail right hemisphere involvement." Ibid., 166. He notes that there is "considerably more flexibility in the human brain in the way that such operations and logical implications can be carried out."

It is thought that weakness of the logical-mathematical abilities is not mainly due to brain diseases but rather is the result of more general deteriorating maladies such as dementia that brings about the decomposition of large portions of the nervous system.

Two electrophysiological investigations reported that both hemispheres are quite involved in solving mathematical problems. A complex, rapidly changing pattern of electrical activity was noted in many areas of both sides of he brain.

It could thus be concluded that logical-mathematical ability is not as autonomous a system as the other types of intelligence, but probably should be considered as some kind of supra- or more general intelligence. Recall the fact that mathematics is the only discipline that stands alone not dependent on any other subject.

Armstrong describes the logical-mathematical abilities as a form of "imageless thinking, characteristic of scientists and higher mathematicians, is hard to describe since there is little that gives it shape or form." Ibid., 95. Physicist W. I. Beveridge was quoted to say: "Physics has reached a stage where it is no longer possible to visualize mechanical analogies representing certain phenomena that can only be expressed in mathematical terms." In other words, physics tends more and more towards mathematics to explain some observed phenomena, and the field of Theoretical Physics is an example. The undergraduate courses of Applied Mathematics (mentioned earlier) deals with physical topics such as Statics and Dynamics.

John Forbes Nash was a Mathematics professor at Princeton. The "A BEAUTIFUL MIND" movie, produced in 2001, described the true personal and academic life of the Nobel laureate.

The genius professor was acknowledged by both his colleagues at the Mathematics Department as well as by his students. He was also happily married. A perfect, in fact, the dream life of any man.

Professor Nash started to get visions that took him adrift. Disillusion intensified, and he began to behave erratically. Things got worse at the university, and students started to make fun of him as he made odd movements in the hallways inside the buildings and on the corridors outside. The Department was so embarrassed that the decision to keep the professor away had to be done.

During this sad episode, Dr. Nash had basically no body to stand beside him but his always loving and supporting wife. She was the pillar when all other pillars collapsed. She believed in him. She stood firmly beside him, and encouraged him.

Gradually Nash started to get himself back together. He fought back the illusive visions and imaginative characters that distracted him.

With his wife's insistence and encouragement, he went back to see the chairman of the Mathematics Department. It was clear that professor Nash had recovered.

The students flocked to seek his help and assistance in their assignments as well as in their research work. His kind heart, and willingness to help became obvious to all faculty, and culminated in him being nominated for the Nobel Prize in Economics.

In 1994, his speech of acceptance of the great honor was both captivating and emotional. Dr. John F. Nash talked about his bouts of mental illness, his recovery and returning back to reality. All the time while he addressed the audience, his attention was totally devoted to his wife sitting in the front row with misty eyes. A great love story between the man with a beautiful mind and the faithful, dedicated wife.

Nash was born in Bluefield, West Virginia on June 13, 1928. He died on May 23, 2015 in Monroe, New Jersey. His most contributions were in the Game Theory, Differential Equations, Inverse Function Theorem, and Geometric Analysis.

CHAPTER 12

THE PERSONAL INTELLIGENCE

The last two types of intelligence are the most difficult to deal with. G. K. Chesterton wrote: "One may understand the cosmos, but never the ego; the self is more distant than any star. Thou shalt love the Lord thy God; but thou shalt not know thyself."

Early in the twentieth century, Sigmund Freud devised the theory of psychoanalysis or the theory of human personality. Its focus is on the development of the individual psyche, "its battles within the individual's immediate family, the struggle for independence, and the manifold anxieties and defenses that attend the human condition." Howard Gardner, Ibid., 251-2. In other words, the key to a healthy life was self-knowledge.

William James, dean of American psychologists and philosophers, had chosen to embrace a more positively oriented form of psychology. He stressed the importance of relationships with other people as a means of gaining ends, and of knowing oneself. James believed that through interaction with others, the individual might undergo change and growth. James influenced the succeeding generation of social scientists such as James M. Baldwin and George H. Mead, who focused on the social origins of knowledge as well as the interpersonal nature of the person's sense of self.

So, whereas Freud stressed the individual's struggles within himself, James advocated that view of knowing the self comes through relationships with others. In other words, Freud's interest was in the person's knowledge of himself. The individual's interest in others was justified chiefly as a better way of gaining further understanding of one's problems, anxieties, wishes, and ultimately, of achieving one's goals.

On the other hand, James's focus fell more on the person's relationship to the outside community. The purpose of self-knowledge was less to promote one's personal goals and more to promote the smooth functioning of the wider community.

For the intrapersonal aspects of an individual, the core capacity at work is access to one's range of effects and emotions. This includes discrimination among these feelings, label them, and draw upon them as a means of understanding and guiding the individual's behavior. Intrapersonal knowledge allows a person to detect his own complex and highly differentiated sets of feelings.

On the other hand, interpersonal intelligence is the "ability to notice and make distinctions among other individuals," particularly "among their moods, temperaments, motivations, and intentions." Gardner, Ibid., 253. This knowledge permits a smart person to read the intentions and desires of many other people, and probably be able to act upon this knowledge by, say, influencing a group of disparate individuals to follow some selected lines. Political and religious leaders possess some highly developed forms of interpersonal intelligence.

More than with any other type of intelligence, intrapersonal and interpersonal intelligence vary considerably from one individual to the other. And because each culture has its own ways of interpreting individual experiences, personal intelligence is highly influenced by systems of meaning that are quite distinct from one another.

When the authors of this work moved to the U.S. In March of 1981, at their early forties, they encountered a distinct culture from the one they lived in before. Body language, hand gestures, facial expressions, and even words convey messages that may or may not be the same as the ones they were used to. An individual from another society needs to be attentive to the symbol system in his/her new environment in order to fit smoothly therein.

The breakdown of personal intelligence also has numerous varieties. What might be an abnormal behavior in one setting can be deemed normal in another culture. Personal intelligence may decline in acuity or assumes aberrant forms.

It is essential to note that the two types of personal intelligence are distinct from one another. Intrapersonal intelligence deals with an individual's examination and knowledge of his feelings. Interpersonal intelligence looks outward, toward the feelings, behavior, and motivation of others.

Each form has an identifiable core, a characteristic pattern of development, neurological representation, and discernible patterns of breakdown.

"The reason for treating these together is … expositional.... These two forms of knowledge are intimately intermingled … with knowledge of one's own person perennially dependent upon the ability to apply lessons learned from the observation of other people, while knowledge of others draws upon the internal discriminations the individual routinely makes." Gardner, Ibid., 255.

Ordinarily, then, both forms of personal intelligence develop simultaneously and reversibly. The individual tries to deploy his knowledge of the personal realm to enhance his own well-being and his relationship to the community.

For some reason, forms of personal intelligence have been largely ignored or minimized by most students of cognition. This occurred in spite of the undeniable fact that these forms of knowledge have tremendous importance in many, if not all, world societies.

Consider a country like Egypt, where the authors of this work had lived for many years. In a nation where bureaucracy has deep roots extending probably for thousands of years, personal relationships are of the utmost significance. Government employees have broad leeway in interpreting and executing rules and regulations that have accumulated and multiplied over the years creating a web of sometimes contradicting documents that can be applied selectively either to benefit or to delay a citizen's request. In that environment having someone who knows someone who is a friend of the employee in charge would make the difference between having your business approved, or having all kinds of obstacles raised against you. Bribery is an alternative avenue to overcome such fictional barriers.

Fortunately, the Egyptian people, by and large, are sociable individuals who enjoy talking and joking. It might be said that the Egyptians' personal intelligence is highly developed whether genetically or as a means of survival. The more people you know and befriend, the easier your life would be.

Not much evidence exists for exceptional individuals in personal realms. This applies to both prodigies or freaks. But this lack might be attributed to the reluctance of psychologists to research this area rather than any difficulties associated with assessing these forms of knowledge.

Every individual develops some balance between the promptings of his own inner feelings and the pressures and expectations of other persons. The sense of self can be traced to two forms of intelligence that every person has the opportunity to develop and to merge.

To put it differently, personal intelligence can be looked at as information-processing capabilities—one directed inward; the other outward. The capacity to know oneself and to know others is an innate part of the human identity just as the ability to know objects or sounds.

From birth, the infant bonds to the mother—a link and an attachment that is an indispensable component of normal growth. During pregnancy, the baby is formed and fed in the mother's womb. After delivery, some of the baby's live tissue remains in the mother's system. Many attribute the mother-baby emotional attachment to this physical connection between the two that seems to continue even after the separation of the two.

For a year or so, the child is disturbed if suddenly

separated from the mother. Gradually, the attachment gets looser as the child realizes that he can return to find the mother there. The lack of this vital bond can wreak havoc in development that shows again in succeeding generations.

Observation of infants by psychologists leaves no doubt that there is a set of universal facial expressions displayed by all normal children. The inference is that there are bodily and brain states associated with these expressions, ranging from excitement and pleasure to pain. The range of bodily states helps to introduce the child to the realm of intrapersonal knowledge. He starts to discover his unique identity.

The child distinguishes his mother from his father, parents from strangers, happy expressions from angry ones. By the age of ten months, "the infant's ability to discriminate among different affective expressions already yields distinctive patterns of brain waves." Gardner, Ibid., 259. The child starts to associate various feelings with certain individuals and circumstances. Feelings of empathy start to show. The child feels sympathetic when he hears or sees another child in pain or crying. He starts to react to his own name, to feel good when he is successful, to experience anxiety when he violates standards set for him by others.

At the age of two to five the child becomes able to refer to himself by saying 'me' or 'mine' and he refers to other individuals using symbols such as 'you' or 'Mom.' Pictures, words, gestures, and numbers become part of the child's life as he comes to know the world symbolically. Physically he reaches the stage of being able to act upon his environment. It can be said that by the age of five, the child is a symbolizing creature.

The child starts to move from living within his moods to the far elaborated set of choices established by society. The dominant culture provides him a whole system of interpretation. He starts to explore some of the different roles played in the community: mother and child, teacher and student, doctor and patient.

Children come to correlate the behavior of other individuals with their own experiences: they identify what provokes anxiety or relaxation, what is positive or negative. In other words, youngsters step into the phase of defining what they are and what they are not.

Theoretical studies of this period of child's life mark the different paths associated with the two types of personal intelligence. Some researchers focus on the child as an isolated individual, a creature set apart, feeling himself different from others, and restricted to his self-centered views. He remains a one-dimensional entity, striving to establish his autonomy from others around him, relatively insensitive to the realm of other persons.

Whereas the intrapersonal-centered opinion of early childhood starts with an isolated person who gradually gets to know about other individuals, the interpersonal approach supposes an innate orientation toward other persons as the only available way for eventually discovering the nature of one's own self.

Howard Gardner tends to think that the two views are, in fact, stressing different aspects of personal development. The child is compelled to watch others as a clue to himself.

The two types of personal intelligence could be viewed as a reversible reaction: intrapersonal talent helps the child to understand himself, which in turn helps him in developing interpersonal knowledge; the latter reinforces his intrapersonal intelligence.

Having reached the school-age, the child has now some concrete mental operations that allow him to relate to others in a more flexible way. He has developed a sense of reciprocity: he envisions things in a certain way because of his own thinking, but he can also apprehend physical and material matters from the points of view of the others around him. The child has reached a stage where a clear distinction exists between self and other, between his own perspective and that of others.

At the age of six, seven, or eight, the child's focus is on the things he can do. With that comes a desire to compete with siblings, tempered with the fear of losing or the appearance of feeling inadequate or unskilled.

The period of middle childhood is the five-year span between the start of school and the beginning of adolescence. Children develop a trend for more social sensitivity and one's competences and weaknesses. A lot of thinking is directed toward cementing one's place within a network of friends. This involves a focus on the interpersonal world. The child feels alone and unhappy if he fails to forge effective friendships with other individuals, and his image of himself suffers.

In adolescence, the person seeks friends who appreciate his insights, knowledge, and sensitivity rather than his wealth or physical strength. The youth welcomes the existence of laws and consider them a necessity for society to function properly, but that mitigating circumstances may be considered in applying such laws.

The adolescent continues his goal of being loved and appreciated by others, but he recognizes that some issues must be kept private.

The turbulent years of adolescence involve a "maturation of knowledge of one's person as well as knowledge of other persons." Gardner, Ibid., 265. So the individual realizes that he must bring together these two forms of personal knowledge into a broader sense. The emerging identity comprises a more complex definition of self and a formulation of what the community needs and expects of him. No wonder this period in life is considered *turbulent both* for the adolescent as well as for the parents.

And the struggle does not stop with adolescence. It continues throughout life even till old age. Adjustments are unavoidable in search of a stage of equilibrium between the individual's own needs and desires while maintaining healthy relationships with the people around him. The intrapersonal knowledge is always in interaction with the interpersonal skills for the person to enjoy a healthy, happy life. The society has a set of constraints on how the person confronts his feelings and idiosyncrasies and still allow smooth and productive functioning with other members of the community.

As difficult as it may be, the ever-changing circumstances enveloping the individual living within one and the same culture is considerably magnified when, and if, he moves to another culture. Here, the additional burden entails knowledge of the new norms of the other culture through continuously observing, watching, and reading about the host society. Then comes the adjustment of the interpersonal skills to conform with those of the new community.

Cultures differ appreciably in their relative emphasis on the intrapersonal or interpersonal intelligence. In Western culture, the focus is on the self, whereas less developed cultures emphasize the society as a whole.

The authors happen to have a first-hand experience in this regard as they moved, at the age of 40, from Egypt to the U.S. back in March of 1981. If given a choice, moving to the West would have been much easier had it took place at an earlier age when the change of behavior is not as hard. Adjustments of one's discriminations to properly suit the adopted new culture takes time and patience as the newcomer persist on observing, learning, and "reading" the signals of other individuals in his milieu. He should develop the skills that will enable him to interpret a social situation correctly and then to start the proper moves in response.

Among the different types of intelligence, the personal realm is the most elusive. It is still an uncertain domain when it comes to how to instruct individuals to develop personal skills. There are no reliable criteria for determining the extent to which training of personal intelligence has been successful.

Some individuals are just born with the talent of understanding one's own feelings as well as the ability to focus on others and the mastery of the social role. Undoubtedly, talent is imperative in developing all types of intelligence, but it is more so concerning the personal intelligence where no clear guidelines exist as to how to develop it or how to measure the success of training in its realm.

A case in point. The authors of this work are both scientists and mathematicians. Their three daughters were expected to follow along the same lines as their parents. The older two got degrees in Chemical Engineering and in Medicine, M.D. The youngest proved different. Since childhood, Shahira was outgoing, smart, and developed friendships as easily as breathing. She was loved by all, and she loved the others. She has a degree in Journalism from William Allen White's school, the University of Kansas. She worked as vice president for marketing and communication for several Kansas associations before starting her own lobbying company. Her studies helped to sharpen her borne skills.

Howard Gardner explains that at the core of personal knowledge, there seems to be "two kinds of information. One is our ability to know other people—to recognize their faces, their voices, and their persons; to react appropriately to them …. The other kind is our sensitivity to our own feelings, wants, and fears, our personal histories." Ibid., 277.

Not all individuals undergo the normal processes of personal development and knowledge of self and others. An autistic child may well have spared computational abilities, particularly in music or mathematics, but is unable to communicate with others in addition to an impaired sense of self. The autistic child has difficulty in knowing others and in using this knowledge to know himself.

On the other hand, some individuals have keen

knowledge of their own feelings but are unable to act upon this knowledge in the presence of others. By definition, this is a case that would be most difficult for anyone to identify.

Brain injury to the dominant cerebral (left) hemisphere may cause a person to become aphasic. A stroke may affect one's own ability to speak but does not necessarily impair personal knowledge. Many of those who have been aphasic but recovered speak of diminished alertness and depression about their condition but never felt to be a different person. He was aware of his own needs and desires and did his best to achieve them. The aphasic's ability to communicate with other persons and to reflect upon his own condition survives intact.

On the other hand, unilateral injury to the right hemisphere does not affect language ability. But the damage causes a significant change in personality and in the modes of relating to others. Ties to other individuals become superficial; there is little interest in personal relationships, scant sense of drive, and little signs of plans for recovery. Perhaps the lack of awareness of their condition is the reason for the poor recovery observed in those with injury to the non-dominant or minor hemisphere.

Evidence tends to suggest that forms of personal intelligence can be destroyed, or spared, in isolation from other kinds of cognition. Furthermore, there are considerable hints in pathological literature that intrapersonal and interpersonal forms of intelligence can be distinguished from one another.

Here a question springs to mind. Can personal intelligence rises up to the level of the other basic and biological intelligences considered in the previous chapters? Gardner believes that "knowledge of self and others ... [is] a more integrated form of intelligence, one more at the behest of the culture and of historical factors, one more truly emergent, one that ultimately comes to control and to regulate more 'primary orders' of intelligence.... personal intelligences... [have] their origins ... in the directly experienced feelings of the individual, ... and in the direct perception of significant other individuals." Ibid., 290.

In general, cultures have to confront the choice of selecting the individual self, the nuclear family, the community, or the nation as the primary unit of analysis. Through this choice, cultures determine, or rather dictate, the degree to which the person peers inward to himself or looks outward to others. Ultimately, there would be some balance between intrapersonal and the interpersonal factors.

In conclusion, the seven types of intelligence can be categorized as follows. The 'object-related' forms of intelligence: spatial, logical-mathematical, and bodily-kinesthetic. These are exerted by the structure and the functions of the specific objects with which persons come into contact. The 'object-free' types of intelligence are language and music. These are not channeled by the physical world but reflect features of the auditory and oral systems. The two personal forms of intelligence are the result of a set of powerful and competing constraints: the existence of one's person; the existence of other individuals; the culture's interpretation of selves.

CHAPTER 13

HIGHER-LEVEL COGNITIVE PROCESSES

The theory of multiple intelligence, MI, does not address cognitive capacities that seem to be of 'higher-level.' These include common sense, originality, metaphorical ability, and wisdom. All of them clearly make use of mental skills, but their broad and general nature render them inexplicable within the confines of the MI theory.

COMMON SENSE is defined by Taylor as "sound judgment derived from experience rather than study." Gardner defines it as "the ability to deal with problems in an intuitive, rapid, and perhaps unexpectedly accurate manner." Ibid., 303.

Dr. Jim Taylor of the University of San Francisco posted on his website on July 12, 2011, an article about common sense. He says that "Common sense is neither common nor sense …. If common sense was common … people wouldn't do a multitude of things that are clearly not good for them …. And common sense isn't real sense, if we define sense as being sound judgment, because relying on experience alone doesn't usually offer enough information to draw reliable conclusions."

Interestingly, the term common sense is often used by people who don't have the real knowledge, expertise, or direct experience to make sound judgments. That is, common sense falls prey to the obvious limits of personal experience.

Taylor recommends the development of a course that deals with scientific thinking and methodology for everyday life that should be a requirement for all students.

The term common sense is customarily invoked by people skilled in the interpersonal domain as well as those gifted in the bodily and spatial intelligence. It is rarely mentioned by individuals skilled in music or mathematics. In other words, it entails the practical application of a small minority of intelligences.

Common sense is also evident in individuals who are able to plan ahead, to exploit opportunities, to guide their destinies and the density of others in a prudent way. Such people have the capacity to bring together a wide amount of seemingly unrelated information and to make it part of a general and successful plan of action.

ORIGINALITY can be defined as the ability to think independently and creatively. An original work implies a quality of being novel or unusual. Merriam Webster defines originality as the freshness of aspect, design, or style. Gardner explains it as "the skill of fashioning an unfamiliar and yet worthy product within a particular realm." Ibid., 304.

Originality or novelty mostly occurs within a single

domain. It is very rare to encounter individuals who are original across the intellectual spectrum.

Early on, most children appear to be engaging in novel or original behavior. This may be attributed to the fact that the child is not really aware of the boundaries between domains. Nor does he have a stake in reaching a solution to a situation or a problem. He does not care about inconsistencies or departures from conventional ideas.

But this originality is not the same as what we expect from a highly skilled person in a field. Genuine novelty appears when an individual has achieved an elaborate experience in the field he has been involved in. Only a person with the necessary skills and comprehensive understanding of the details of the field can sense where a real innovation will lie and how best to achieve it.

It is also possible that the seeds of originality are planted since early in life and are reflected in basic temperament or personality. Such individuals are likely candidates for original products even if they have not attained the highest level of knowledge in their field. In contrast, persons who lack these personal attributes will never be original even if they reach the top of their field.

Several studies were carried out on the 'creative' personality. Personality traits such as ego strength and courage to defy tradition describe the outstanding creative persons; they also help to explain why scores on creativity measures do not correlate with scores on more conventional tests of intellectual strengths—at least beyond a certain level of IQ.

METAPHORICAL ABILITY A metaphor is a figure

of speech that refers, for rhetorical effect, to one thing by mentioning another thing. It may provide clarity or identify hidden similarities between two ideas. The expression that 'All the world's a stage' expresses a metaphor because the world is not literally a stage. By asserting that the world is a stage, Shakespeare uses points of comparison between the world and a stage to convey an understanding of the mechanics of the world and the behavior of the people within it.

The capacity to make a metaphor or to perceive analogies cut across various intellectual domains in order to forge such hidden connections.

Metaphorical ability may be defined as the capacity to integrate diverse intelligences. Aristotle believed that the skill to create metaphors is the very sign of genius.

But it is also possible—even highly likely—that the skill to discern analogies exits within certain domains. Practitioners get skilled at finding out relationships within their chosen domains.

A question springs to mind. Could it be that there is a form of metaphoric capacity, separate from other types of intelligence, that some people have developed to a high level so that they can apply it upon particular intellectual domains? Gardner does not find sufficient evidence to assign a separate form of intelligence to the metaphorical skills. Except for the proven existence of a developed end-state, metaphoric intelligence does not show those signs that have proved essential in the identification of other types of intelligence.

It may be safe to say that people who are good at

metaphorizing have developed this skill in one or more domains over their general learning process but then reached this stage where they feel sufficiently secure with this ability that they can apply it in the domains in which they are involved. Top metaphorizers will discern analogies virtually everywhere.

WISDOM Gardner refers to wisdom as the power of 'general synthesizing.' It is a type of intelligence that one expects from "an older person who has had a wide range of critical experiences in his earlier life and can now apply them appropriately and judiciously, in the proper circumstances." Ibid., 309.

Individuals who possess some combination of common sense and originality in one or more domains coupled with a seasoned metaphorizing capacity may be marked as wise men. The person can draw upon these skills to come up with well-motivated courses of action. But, in reality, it is very rare for a human being to come up with a convincing formulation, or a perfect plan of action.

This may not be surprising since man is finite in both his knowledge and understanding. The Word of God warns against trusting in one's own wisdom. PROVERBS, 3:7 says Be not wise in thine own eyes: fear the LORD, and depart from evil.

True wisdom comes only from the Creator of the universe. JAMES 1:5 explains, "If any of you lack wisdom, let him ask God, that giveth to all men liberally, and upbraideth not; and it shall be given unto him."

PROVERBS, 1:2-3, 5 states, "To know wisdom and instruction; to perceive the words of understanding; To receive the instruction of wisdom, justice, and judgment, and equity .... A wise man will hear, and will increase learning; a man of understanding shall attain unto wise counsels."

Implied in the above verses is a spirit of humility and a belief in our LORD.

ECCLESIASTES, 2:26 says For God giveth to a man that is good in his sight wisdom, and knowledge, and joy .... The Bible emphasizes the same principle in PROVERBS, 2:7 He [The LORD] layeth up sound wisdom for the righteous: he is a buckler to them that work uprightly. PROVERBS, 1:7 explains The fear of the LORD is the beginning of knowledge: but fools despise wisdom and instruction.

God, in His mercy, declares wisdom to men in no uncertain terms. PROVERBS, 1:20 states Wisdom crieth without; she uttereth her voice in the streets. PROVERBS, 2:2 tells So that you incline thine ear unto wisdom, and apply thine heart to understanding. PROVERBS, 2:10-11 says Man when wisdom entereth into thine heart and knowledge is pleasant unto your soul; Discretion shall preserve thee, understanding shall keep thee.

PROVERBS, 3:13 says Happy is the man that findeth wisdom, and the man that getteth understanding.

The above are just some of the Bible verses that explicitly mention the word *wisdom.* However, from GENESIS to REVELATION, the Word of God is all wisdom.

EXTRASENSORY PERCEPTION? In the 1930s, Dr. Joseph B. Rhine of Duke University started the study of extrasensory perception (ESP)--the subjective science of parapsychology. He championed the idea to the point where a department of parapsychology was established at the university.

In the middle 1980s interest was renewed in the subject and became "one of the fastest-growing fields of academic research in our universities today." Billy Graham, ANGELS, Word Books, Waco, Texas, 1986, 22. Scientists probed every conceivable frontier for ESP possibilities. Some serious intellectual and scientific studies were carried out. The subject became immensely popular because "many of its aggressive proponents profess to be nonreligious. It has gained even more widespread respectability in communist societies ... then here in the United States." Ibid., 22.

ESP serves as a 'substitute religion' in some cases in spite of the fact that it has been used primarily to influence and manipulate people.

CHAPTER 14

UNSEEN AND INVISIBLE INTELLIGENCE

The previous chapters discussed the different types of intelligence in addition to some higher-level cognitive processes. Investigative studies could identify associations between the various types of intelligence and specific locations within the brain. All this falls within the natural, material world.

But is there an unseen type of 'intelligence' that belongs to the supernatural? An intelligence that contributes to man's decisions but is undetected by our equipment, experiment, or senses? The late Billy Graham believes there is such an intelligence.

"Today some hard-nosed scientists lend credence to the scientific probability of angels when they admit the likelihood of unseen and invisible intelligence." ANGELS, Ibid., 30.

Before going on in a discussion of this type of intelligence we may refer to some well-known, long proven scientific facts. First, our eyes can only see objects within a relatively minimal range of wavelengths. Scientists identify the visible spectrum (light) as the waves with a wavelength that falls between 4,000 and 7,000 angstrom units. (One-angstrom unit equals 1/100000000 of a centimeter). Morris Hein and Leo R. Best, COLLEGE CHEMISTRY, Brooks/Cole Publishing Co., Monterrey, California, 1980, 399.

Visible light is just one part of the Electromagnetic Radiation Spectrum which covers the range from Gamma radiation, to X-Rays, to Ultraviolet light, to the Visible range, to the Infrared radiation, to the Microwaves, to the Radio waves. Each type covers a range of a specified wavelength. The Gamma radiation starts with a wavelength of 10 to the power of -11 cm or 1/100000000000 of a cm. At the other end of the spectrum, Radio waves have a wavelength of 1,000 cm (or longer).

A look at the range of the Electromagnetic Radiation Spectrum (1X10 to -13 of a meter up to 10 meters) reveals that our sight covers but a really small range (4X10 to -7 up to 7X10 to -7 meters) of the spectrum. Our eyes can not see Gamma rays, X-Rays, Infrared radiation, but all of them are present around us (and some can be generated by the proper equipment).

The point here is that our abilities to see are limited. If angels are existent (and they are), we can not see them unless they choose to make themselves seen by man.

Angels "appear and reappear …. While angels may become visible by choice, our eyes are not constructed to see them ordinarily more than we can see the dimensions of a nuclear field, the structure of atoms, or the electricity that flows through copper wiring. Our ability to sense reality is limited: The deer of the forest far surpass our human capacity in their keenness of smell. Bats possess a phenomenally sensitive built-in radar system. ...geese possess sophisticated guidance systems that appear to border on the supernatural." Billy Graham, Ibid., 30-31.

Second, our ears can only detect but a limited range of the audio spectrum. Billy Graham, Ibid., 30, writes, "Angels speak." But can we always 'hear' them?

The human audio spectrum has a frequency that ranges from 20 to 20,000 Hz or cycles/second. Bats can hear sound waves of frequencies of up to 110,000 Hz, and dogs have a hearing range of 67 to 45,000 Hz. Sound waves with frequencies higher than 20,000 Hz are called ultrasound waves (they can attain frequencies of 200 MHz or 200 million cycles/second depending on the medium they travel through).

Just like our sight, our hearing is limited. When angels speak, we are unable to hear them unless they choose to make their voices audible to man.

"Angels never draw attention to themselves but ascribe glory to God and press His message upon the hearers as a delivering and sustaining word of the higher order.... For, after all, God has given His angels charge of you, to guard you in all your ways." Ibid., 31.

Graham wrote that he received many reports from many places from around the world telling of visitors of the angelic order appearing, ministering, fellowshipping, and disappearing.

John Calvin, in his INSTITUTES, said: "The angels are the dispensers and administrators of the Divine beneficence toward us: they regard our safety, undertake our defense, direct our ways, and exercise a constant solicitude that no evil befall us."

The Bible tells of angels as oracles of God, who gives divine or authoritative decisions and bring messages from God to man. To fulfill this role, angels have not infrequently assumed a visible, human form.

Whether we see them or not, God, in His love for man, has created a vast host of angels to help accomplish His will in the world. As believers in the Almighty and His Son, Jesus Christ, we can have "confidence that the angels of God will watch over us and assist us because we belong to Him." Graham, Ibid., 37.

Can anything compare with these unseen and invisible intelligences? The powerful angels accompany and protect the man in his life experiences.

However, we should not confuse angels with the Holy Spirit. Angels do not dwell in men; the Holy Spirit seals them and indwells them after He has regenerated them. "The Holy Spirit is all-knowing, all present, and all-powerful. Angels are mightier than men, but they are not gods, and they do not possess the attributes of the Godhead." Ibid., 33.

Only the Holy Spirit convicts man of sin, righteousness, and judgment. Angels are messengers of God who serve men as ministering spirits, HEBREWS, 1:14.

The glorious Holy Spirit can be everywhere at the same time, but no angel can be in more than one place at any specific moment.

But angels are in close contact with all that is happening on earth. Their knowledge of earthly matters exceeds that of men. God uses angels to work out the destinies of men and nations. Angels probably "know things about us that we do not know about ourselves. And because they are ministering spirits, they will always use this knowledge for our good." Graham. Ibid., 43.

In 1987 the authors took their family on a trip from Topeka, Kansas to Dallas to visit some relatives. At the time, our daughters ranged in age from 17 to seven years. It was in December right before Christmas.

Somewhere after Wichita, Kansas, on Interstate 35, it started to snow that turned into sleet. Though the conditions forced a slowing down, the 240D Mercedes suddenly left the two-lane-southbound highway and skidded on the low-lying median. Luckily there were no cars behind or beside ours. The vehicle, while skidding, made a 180-degree turn and ended up facing the north. I got out of the car to see and think about how to get back on the road.

Within seconds, a dark blue pick-up truck stopped on the shoulder, and its driver came directly towards me and said: get in the car. Single-handedly he pushed the car (with the five people inside), and I steered it back onto the road.

I got out of the car and sought to thank the 'gentleman' for his great help and courtesy. But he and the pick-up truck disappeared before I had any chance even to shake his hands.

Was 'he' an angel? The guardian angel? I am confident he was. Can I prove that? No. Only faith supports the hypothesis.

In one of his recent sermons, Dr. David Jeremiah said: God can not use a man greatly until He hurts him deeply. The messengers of God know the earthly matters.

CHAPTER 15

CONTROLLING THE HUMAN MIND – ARTIFICIALLY?

David Ambrose is the author of the novel THE DISCREET CHARM OF CHARLIE MONK, Warner Books, New York, NY, 2000.

The fiction work of Ambrose describes how a group of powerful people funded a research project that aimed at planting memories in the mind of an individual. If man is able to control this three-pound organ, called the brain, of another person, the latter is no longer a free entity with the ability to choose but a robot-like creature in the form of a human being.

The main intent of the project was to have a 'killing machine' that can handle some dangerous, critical assignments. These might involve killing one or a group of unwanted persons. A smart, fast-moving, powerful man would be the appropriate choice.

But the project had further ambitions. Since field situations require strength and fast movements, why not choose a chimpanzee instead of a human being. Manipulating some human genes might lead to the required qualities.

Chimpanzees are strong and vicious. Even their keepers can never get "within striking distance of a full-grown chimpanzee. He is about eight times stronger than any human being." Ibid., 173. A full-grown male chimpanzee weighs over two hundred pounds.

Gorillas were not selected. Several reasons made gorillas not the first choice for the job. They are less intelligent and less aggressive than chimpanzees. More crucial, they are not as closely related to humans. "The difference between our DNA and the chimpanzee is one point six percent. Between chimpanzees and gorillas, it is two point three— which means that chimps are genetically closer to humans than they are to gorillas." Ibid., 174. In fact, chimpanzees are practically human already, according to Ambrose, except for that one point six percent.

Research has shown that the difference in DNA between humans and chimpanzees is not in the brain. Their brains are slightly smaller than humans but not significantly. The left hemisphere of the human brain is the dominant half, but this is because we have developed speech and sequential thought. Chimpanzees communicate among themselves effectively but on a fairly basic scale. Few have been taught sign language. In general, they have quite a visual sense. But their inability to speak deprived them of achieving progress akin to that of the human race.

And here comes Charlie. He was orphaned early in life and lived in an orphanage. He was smart and had the ability to move fast—very fast. Not surprisingly, Charlie got in trouble. The orphanage sent him to one school after the other for a total of six or seven schools. He hadn't learned one thing that whole time. "Just an endless round of fights or punishment and truancy and more fights." Ibid., 46.

Kathy Ryan was also in the orphanage and love developed between Kathy and Charlie. One morning they ran off together. All they had was just the clothes they wore and some change in their pockets.

Being in love and at the age of sixteen, Charlie and Kathy sought some location for privacy. They were caught trying to jump a freight train. Charlie fought against two cops who were bigger than him. His dogged fight against authorities didn't end as he wished. They had him cuffed and placed in a police cell. An armored van, used for carrying prisoners to jail, took Charlie back to the orphanage.

There he was left alone in a room with three guards who looked like gorillas. They told him they were responsible for 'security' in the orphanage and that they were going to teach him a lesson he would never forget. Except it did not all go their way.

He was able to hurt one of them very badly before the other two used baseball bats to beat him with brutal force. After that, they had thrown him in the 'hole.' He had nothing to eat or drink for twenty-four hours. As the numbness wore off, the pain felt worse.

Finally, they dragged him out and had him checked by a doctor. He was put in another prison van and taken on a long drive. The van passed through the gates of someplace that looked like a private ranch or a big park. Charlie could see young men working out and playing all kinds of sports. It looked like a training camp.

Charlie got all the training deemed necessary for him

to carry out some critical assignments. The raw talent and in-born intelligence of Charlie were even more developed and sharpened by the specialized training at the Farm.

The communication between Charlie and the higher-ups was achieved through a handler who called himself Control.

And control he did.

The orphan boy, now a grown-up who is well trained to kill, executed some successful dangerous jobs. One assignment for Charlie was to be dropped from an airplane on an embassy where terrorists had held a number of hostages. Among those held was a young senator who would be running for vice president in three years' time. Charlie's job was to put a bullet through the young senator's head. He did his job perfectly.

Susan Fleming was a medical doctor married to John, who was also a doctor. Unlike her husband, she went into research. Her work was about the human mind.

Brian Kay has a memory problem. He forgets some things that have happened recently, but he does remember others. While in hospital, his wife visits him every day, but every morning he sees her coming into his room he tells her that he missed seeing her and was worried something had happened to her. She gently reminds him that she was in the hospital with him the day before. This went on every day.

In one of her lectures, Dr. Susan Fleming explained to her audience the medical condition of Brian Kay.

"A virus attacked that part of Brian Kay's brain that processed sense perceptions into short- and long-term memory. Consequently, he became trapped in an eternal present, with no way of translating his moment-by-moment perceptions into any kind of meaningful narrative that he could then store in the way that normal memory is stored." Ibid., 32.

Kay could only remember the things he had learned before the virus attacked his brain. His childhood, college, marriage, and teaching career all remained intact. But the illness had opened a gulf between the past and the present moment as well as each successive present moment. Interestingly, his intelligence has remained the same and undiminished. But the problem is that he can not learn, because once the information is over, he can not transfer anything from perception into memory that can be retrieved at any time later on.

Research by Dr. Fleming led her to develop a noninvasive procedure that allows researchers to send a visual image directly into the brain, "bypassing the eye … [and] also bypass that part of the brain which would normally process visual stimuli into memory. … it remains a long way from a full cure, but it is a start." Ibid., 34.

Susan Fleming needed funding to continue her research. Her father, Amery Hyde, was a retired diplomat who had many connections. The Pilgrim Foundation approached her. She asked her father to 'ask around' about this corporation. Her father recommended it.

Out of the blue Latimer West, the Foundation's CEO, called Susan one day and made an appointment to see her. She was trying to avoid the big drug companies who tend to tie up the researcher for life. An agreement was put in force that guaranteed to fund of Dr. Fleming's research by the Pilgrim Foundation.

In her first visit to the Foundation, Susan was treated very poorly. A guard accompanied her to a security holding area that had no furniture. Then she was shown into an office where a petty bureaucrat sat behind a desk. He did not bother to stand on his feet when she entered. In fact, he did not even look up from the document he was reading. After a non-friendly conversation with that person, Latimer West entered the room without her hearing. He had degrees in medicine and in accounting.

In West's office, Susan found out that the contract she signed with Pilgrim Foundation gives the latter free hand in directing and using *all* further research carried out by Dr. Fleming. After a physical confrontation between the two, two guards entered the room and dragged her away, pinning her arms behind her back. She calmed down after a few minutes.

When Susan insisted on having the final word in directing her future research work, her son was abducted. Her father called her at West's office and stressed to her that she must do as they say.

Dr. Fleming was flown to what looked like a military installation in California. She was made aware that the Pilgrim Foundation has already taken certain aspects of her work further than she ever envisaged. West, however, admitted that his researchers had problems with the visual memory of the subject—Charlie. Susan is expected to work on solving the obstacle. It was made clear to her that her help is the condition for getting her son back.

Charlie was injured during his bold job at the embassy and the killing of the young senator. While recovering in the hospital, his mind drifted into thinking about Kathy Ryan, his first love at the orphanage with whom he escaped to freedom. At least this is what he thought. Her image was so clear that he opened his eyes and tried to sit up. Even the brutal pain "that shot through him didn't dislodge the picture from his mind's eye." Ibid., 98. Charlie wondered how could he have forgotten that face that he had loved so deeply, and then suddenly remember it now?

Susan had done what they had asked of her, but it was not over yet. She had to be on standby in case anything else important or urgent came up.

After Charlie recovered, he was sent home. But he was always kept under surveillance. His leisure time was spent on his hobby of painting.

One morning while he was painting and enjoying the scenery around him, he saw a woman approaching him. "It took him a long moment to speak the name of the woman who stood before him." Ibid., 109. "Kathy," he said at last. After a short conversation, Charlie found out that the woman was married and her husband had died. Although she claimed that she did remember Charlie, her response to his obvious excitement at seeing her after such a long time did puzzle him. (It turned out later that the woman was not Kathy Ryan but Dr. Fleming herself who managed to implant information in Charlie's visual memory for him to see her as Kathy.)

Charlie Monk was assigned some other jobs that he executed quite successfully. Control arranged for Charlie to meet the woman he thought to be Kathy. When Charlie pressed her to tell him what is going on and why she keeps denying him, she finally said, "I am not Kathy. There is no Kathy Ryan. My name is Susan—Dr. Susan Fleming." When he tried to object, she lifted a small black object in her hand. "A strip of light opened horizontally across the center of his vision." Ibid., 141. Charlie could hear the voices of other people present in the room who were talking *about* him, not *to* him. He was placed in some kind of a silvery suit with cables of differing thickness attached to various parts of it.

Later, alone in the room, he looked at his hands. His hand was an ape's hand. His face was similarly rough and covered with hair; his lips were wide and thin with a leathery edge. Instead of a nose, he had a small mound in the middle of his face. They removed the silvery suit and put him in a cage. A mirror opposite his cage showed a full-grown chimpanzee.

His cage led to a vast open space with tall trees of oak and beech. Groups of chimpanzees were scattered singly or in groups. Charlie was in a zoo. The male leader of the group forced Charlie into an altercation which he lost. Charlie was essentially left alone by the other chimpanzees who showed respect to their new leader.

Having made a lot of progress in her research project, Dr. Fleming went to talk to Latimer West in his office. She wanted out and her son back. He strongly refused to stop the project; her work is not yet completed.

Susan went to Charlie's cage. She brought an easel with a fresh canvas, a palette of paints and brushes. He dipped the brush in a whorl of green paint then touched it to the canvas. Although he could not speak, he could at least write.

But he realized he could not write. Yet Dr. Fleming realized that Charlie can still understand. He also remembered everything that they did to him. She was disappointed. "This was not supposed to happen," she said.

Researchers sought to find out if the chimpanzee brain was capable of doing what they wanted it to do. They were trying to "create a human look-alike—stronger and faster than any man on earth, and totally obedient to his masters. They were planning to make him out of a genetically mutated chimpanzee." Ibid., 189.

The goal was to take a "fertilized egg, genetically modify it, then implant it in the womb of a female chimpanzee. The baby, a male, will be taken from her at birth. He will be reared in a lab in isolation. When he is about eight years old, he will look like a fully grown human being. He won't know he is any different from the rest of them." Ibid., 189.

The key to brainwashing isn't just wiping memories. It is planting new ones. The hardest kind of memory to plant is visual memory. They sought to plant visual images of things the brain had never seen before and yet would recognize when they were encountered in reality.

Yes, it is all fiction. But the point is if you control the mind, the body will follow. This three-pound organ is marvelous in its design, components, and functions.

Printed in the United States
By Bookmasters